THE HOLY SPIRIT

ALL WHO ARE LED BY THE SPIRIT OF GOD ARE SONS OF GOD

EDWARD D. ANDREWS

THE HOLY SPIRIT

All Who Are Led by the Spirit of God Are Sons of God

Edward D. Andrews

Christian Publishing House

Cambridge, Ohio

CHRISTIAN
PUBLISHING
HOUSE

FOUNDED 2005

THE HOLY SPIRIT: All Who Are Led by the Spirit of God Are Sons of God by Edward D. Andrews

ISBN-10: 1949586170

ISBN-13: 978-1949586176

Table of Contents

Preface

The journey of exploring the Holy Spirit's role and work in the lives of believers is one that promises to be both enlightening and transformative. This book, "THE HOLY SPIRIT: All Who Are Led by the Spirit of God Are Sons of God," aims to provide a comprehensive and in-depth understanding of the Holy Spirit's presence and activity from the earliest pages of Scripture to the present day.

The inspiration for this work comes from a deep desire to equip believers with the knowledge and tools necessary to live Spirit-filled lives that honor God. The Holy Spirit's work is multifaceted, encompassing guidance, empowerment, conviction, and transformation. As believers, we are called to walk by the Spirit, allowing His influence to permeate every aspect of our lives.

Throughout the pages of this book, we will delve into the scriptural foundations that reveal the Holy Spirit's character and operations. From the Old Testament narratives to the New Testament teachings, we will uncover the consistent and powerful work of the Spirit in guiding God's people, empowering them for service, and transforming their lives to reflect the character of Christ.

In addition to the core chapters, the appendices address several significant and often controversial topics related to the Holy Spirit, such as speaking in tongues, snake handling, and the preservation of the biblical texts. These discussions aim to provide clarity and biblical insight, helping believers navigate these issues with confidence and understanding.

I would like to express my heartfelt gratitude to Z. T. Sweeney for his pioneering work on the Holy Spirit. His insights and contributions have been invaluable in shaping a deeper understanding of the Spirit's role in the life of the believer. Sweeney's dedication to exploring the depths of the Holy Spirit's work has provided a foundation upon which this book builds.

As you embark on this journey through the pages of "THE HOLY SPIRIT: All Who Are Led by the Spirit of God Are Sons of God," it is my hope and prayer that you will be encouraged, equipped, and empowered to live a life led by the Spirit. May this exploration deepen your relationship with God and enhance your understanding of His divine presence and work in your life.

Edward D. Andrews

Author of 220+ books

Introduction

Understanding the role and work of the Holy Spirit is crucial for every believer. The Holy Spirit, as the third person of the Trinity, is integral to the Christian faith and life. Yet, misconceptions and misunderstandings about the Holy Spirit abound, often leading to confusion and division within the church. This book seeks to clarify and illuminate the truth about the Holy Spirit, grounded firmly in Scripture and the historical context of the early church.

The Holy Spirit's work is evident throughout the Bible, from the very beginning in Genesis to the closing verses of Revelation. In the Old Testament, the Spirit of God moved powerfully in creation, inspired the prophets, and anointed leaders to accomplish God's purposes. In the New Testament, the Holy Spirit's work is even more pronounced, especially in the life and ministry of Jesus Christ, the apostles, and the early church. Understanding these foundations is essential for appreciating the Spirit's ongoing work today.

This book is structured to provide a comprehensive exploration of the Holy Spirit's role. Each chapter focuses on different aspects of the Spirit's work, providing biblical exegesis and practical insights. You will discover how the Holy Spirit was active in the Old Testament, the divinity and personhood of the Spirit, and the Spirit's influence on key figures such as John the Baptist and Jesus Christ.

Moreover, the book delves into the Holy Spirit's transformative power in the lives of the apostles and the early church. It examines how the Spirit guided, empowered, and sustained the first believers, enabling them to spread the gospel and establish the church despite intense opposition and persecution.

An essential part of this study is understanding the practical implications for believers today. The Holy Spirit is not merely a historical figure confined to the pages of Scripture but is active and present in the lives of believers now. This book aims to help readers recognize and cultivate the Spirit's presence, live in accordance with the Spirit's guidance, and avoid grieving the Spirit.

The appendices address specific, often controversial topics related to the Holy Spirit, such as speaking in tongues and snake handling. These sections are designed to provide clear, biblically sound answers to these questions, helping believers navigate these issues with wisdom and discernment.

THE HOLY SPIRIT

Throughout this journey, my hope is that you will gain a deeper understanding of the Holy Spirit and His vital role in your life. The Spirit's work is transformative, empowering, and essential for living a victorious Christian life. As you read, may you be inspired to yield more fully to the Spirit's leading, grow in the fruit of the Spirit, and live out your faith with renewed vigor and conviction.

CHAPTER 1 The Holy Spirit and the Old Testament

The first pages of Scripture already confront us with the reality that God does not act at a distance. He creates, orders, sustains, and directs through His Spirit. Long before the outpouring at Pentecost, long before the apostles spoke in other languages, the Spirit of God was already active in powerful, purposeful ways in the history of Israel.

This chapter will show that the Old Testament presents the Holy Spirit as:

God's active power in creation and preservation.

- The One who equips leaders, craftsmen, judges, kings, and elders.

- The One who inspires prophets and preserves God's revelation.
- The One whose work anticipates, but does not yet fully grant, the blessings of the new covenant.

At the same time, we must be very clear about what the Old Testament does not teach. It does not teach that every believer under the old covenant experienced a personal, continuous indwelling of the Holy Spirit in the sense often claimed in modern charismatic circles. It does not present the Spirit as cleansing the heart from sin in an ongoing, internal way before the completed work of Christ and the full new covenant realities. Rather, the Old Testament consistently presents the Spirit of God as the divine power of Jehovah acting in history, especially through chosen individuals, and as the source of revelation that would prepare the way for the Messiah and the apostolic message.

To understand the Holy Spirit today, we must first see clearly how He worked then. Only by grasping the Old Testament patterns can we accurately trace the line of God's plan from creation to Christ to the completed inspired Scriptures that now guide the church.

The Spirit of God in the Old Testament: Names, Terms, and Emphasis

In the Old Testament the Spirit is rarely called "the Holy Spirit." The most common expressions are "the Spirit of God" and "the Spirit of Jehovah." The basic Hebrew word is *ruach*, a term that can mean "wind," "breath," or "spirit," depending on the context. Scripture uses this same term for the wind that blows, the breath that gives life, the human spirit, and the powerful activity of God Himself.

This variety in usage is not confusion. It highlights a consistent idea: *ruach* refers to invisible force that produces visible effects. You cannot see the wind, but you can see trees bending. You cannot see breath, but you can watch a chest rise and fall. In the same way, you cannot see the Spirit of God as a visible "thing," but you can see what He does in creation, in history, and in human lives.

The Old Testament uses explicit expressions for God's Spirit in dozens of texts scattered across the Law, the historical books, the Psalms, and the prophets. In many of these, the Spirit is clearly active: He "comes upon" people, "fills" them, "rests" on them, or is "poured out." Yet the Old Testament seldom pauses to explain the Spirit in abstract theological terms. It simply shows what He does.

Where the New Testament speaks more often of the Holy Spirit in relation to the heart, the conscience, and the inner life of believers, the Old Testament tends to present the Spirit's work in terms of:

- Creation and ordering of the world.
- Empowering particular men and women for particular tasks.
- Giving and guarding prophetic revelation.
- Anticipating a future age when God's Spirit would be poured out more broadly.

This difference in emphasis does not show two different Spirits, but two stages in God's one plan. The same Spirit who hovered over the waters in Genesis empowered Bezalel to build the tabernacle, strengthened David for kingship, moved Isaiah to prophesy, and later raised Jesus from the dead and guided the apostles in writing the New Testament.

The Spirit and the Created Order

The Spirit of God in Creation

The opening words of the Bible already introduce the Spirit:

"The earth was without form and empty, and darkness was over the surface of the deep, and the Spirit of God was moving over the surface of the waters" (Genesis 1:2).

The phrase "moving over" can be understood as hovering or brooding, like a bird over its nest. The picture is not of a distant God watching but of God's own Spirit actively involved in taking what is formless and empty and preparing it to be ordered, fruitful, and good.

Several truths are grounded here:

First, creation is not a random accident. The Spirit of God is personally engaged. What is chaotic becomes structured; what is empty becomes full; what is dark is prepared for light. This is the pattern of God's work through His Spirit throughout Scripture.

Second, the Spirit's work in creation shows His divine power. Only God can take "formless and empty" and bring about a world suitable for human habitation, a world in which His purposes can unfold.

Third, this foundational text already links the Spirit of God with life and order. Later, when the Bible speaks of God renewing and sustaining creation, the same pattern appears.

Psalm 104, a creation psalm, says of living creatures, "You send forth your spirit, they are created, and you renew the face of the ground" (Psalm 104:30). When God "sends forth" His Spirit, life comes into being; when He withdraws, life returns to the dust. Here again the Spirit of God is the divine life-giving power that sustains the world He made.

Job gives an even more personal perspective: "The Spirit of God has made me, and the breath of the Almighty gives me life" (Job 33:4, UASV). Human life is not self-explaining. It is not the result of blind forces. It is the result of God's Spirit at work. The phrase "has made me" does not mean Job was directly created in a miraculous way separate from ordinary birth, but that behind the processes of life stands the direct activity of God's Spirit.

Job 26:13 adds, "By his spirit the heavens are made beautiful." The picture is that the starry skies, the ordered heavens, the constellations—what we see when we look up at night—are not the result of chance, but of the Spirit's work in arranging, ordering, and sustaining the universe.

Taken together, these passages show that the Old Testament presents the Spirit of God as the divine, life-giving, ordering power in creation. The universe is not merely made by God and then left alone; it is constantly dependent on His Spirit.

The Spirit of God and Human Life

The Old Testament also connects God's Spirit with human life in a way that excludes the idea of an immortal soul in the Greek philosophical sense. The human being does not possess an inherently immortal spiritual part. Instead, a human is a soul, a living person, brought to life when God's breath, His life-giving spirit, animates the body.

Genesis 2:7 tells us that Jehovah formed man from the dust of the ground and breathed into his nostrils the breath of life, and man became a living soul. The man was not given an immortal soul; he became a soul—a living person—when God's life-breath animated him.

When that spirit, that God-given breath of life, is withdrawn, the person dies and returns to the dust. Ecclesiastes 12:7 describes this at death: "the dust returns to the earth as it was, and the spirit returns to God who gave it." This "spirit" here is not a conscious, immortal being floating upward; it is the life-force returning to the Giver, and the person ceases to exist as a living self until a future resurrection.

The connection between the Spirit of God and human life presses two truths on us:

First, our existence is entirely dependent on Jehovah. Every breath, every heartbeat, every moment of life depends on the Spirit of God who gives and sustains life.

Second, this life is temporary under the curse of sin. That is why the Spirit's work in creation and preservation must eventually be joined to God's saving plan in Christ, which includes resurrection and a future world where death is no more.

The Spirit and Humanity Before the Flood

Genesis 6 shows the Spirit of God not only as Creator, but as a moral Pleader with a rebellious world. In Genesis 6:3 we read, "Then Jehovah said, 'My Spirit shall not strive with man forever, inasmuch as he also is flesh; nevertheless his days shall be one hundred and twenty years.'"

This verse shows several key points.

First, the Spirit of God is not merely a power; He is a moral agent who "strives" with human beings. His work is not only to create and sustain but also to confront. He presses upon people the reality of God's will and the seriousness of sin.

Second, this striving came through revelation and preaching. In the days before the Flood, Noah is called "a preacher of righteousness"

(2 Peter 2:5). As Noah warned his generation, the Spirit of God was striving with that corrupt world through the preached message. The Spirit did not mysteriously work apart from the word; He worked through the word, using the message to press upon hearts the need to turn from wickedness.

Third, the statement "My Spirit shall not strive with man forever" shows that the striving of the Spirit may cease when people continually refuse to respond. God set a limit, giving that generation a defined period before the judgment of the Flood. When that period ended, the striving of the Spirit ended, and the judgment fell.

This provides a serious lesson for every age. When the Spirit speaks through the Word of God, through faithful preaching and teaching, stubborn refusal can lead to a point at which God's striving ends and only judgment remains. The Holy Spirit is patient, but He is not endlessly ignored without consequence.

The Spirit and Theocratic Leadership in Israel

The Spirit of God and National Leadership

After the Flood and after the call of Abraham, the Spirit of God is frequently associated with God's chosen leaders—the men who guided Israel under the theocratic arrangement.

In the wilderness period, Moses faced the weight of leading a vast and often stubborn people. Jehovah told him to appoint seventy elders. Numbers 11:25 says, "Then Jehovah came down in the cloud and spoke to him; and he took of the Spirit that was upon him and put him upon the seventy men, the elders; and when the Spirit rested upon them, they prophesied, but they did not do it again."

Several truths stand out.

The Spirit was already upon Moses in a unique way, equipping him for the immense task of leading and judging the people. Jehovah did not give a separate Spirit, but "took of the Spirit that was upon him and put him upon the seventy men." This shows a shared enabling, not divided deity.

When the Spirit rested on these elders, they briefly prophesied, giving an outward sign of the Spirit's presence. However, the text carefully notes that this unusual manifestation did not become a permanent, repeated experience. The prophetic outburst was a sign that the Spirit had indeed equipped them; it was not a continual phenomenon.

The purpose of this distribution of the Spirit was practical: to enable spiritual and administrative leadership in the congregation of Israel.

A similar pattern appears with the judges whom Jehovah raised up to deliver Israel from oppression. Judges 3:10 says of Othniel, "The Spirit of Jehovah came upon him, and he judged Israel. When he went out to war, Jehovah gave Cushan-rishathaim king of Mesopotamia into his hand."

The Spirit's coming upon Othniel did not mean Othniel became sinless or had an inner, permanent, sanctifying indwelling. It meant God empowered him for a specific task: to lead Israel in battle and deliver the nation.

Other judges show the same pattern. The Spirit of Jehovah came upon Gideon, upon Jephthah, and repeatedly upon Samson. These men were far from perfect in character, but they were instruments whom the Spirit empowered for particular acts of deliverance. Their moral faults show clearly that Spirit-empowerment for a task is not the same as moral transformation of the heart.

The Spirit of God and Kingship

Later, under the monarchy, the Spirit's relation to kings becomes especially prominent.

When Saul was chosen as Israel's first king, the prophet Samuel told him that the Spirit of Jehovah would come mightily upon him and he would prophesy (1 Samuel 10:6). The passage reports that "God changed his heart" in the sense of equipping him for his role, and the Spirit came upon him so that he prophesied with a group of prophets. Again, this prophetic experience was a sign that the Spirit had empowered Saul for his royal task.

However, Saul's later disobedience and hardening of heart led to a different outcome. 1 Samuel 16:14 states, "Now the Spirit of Jehovah departed from Saul, and an evil spirit from Jehovah terrorized him." Here we see that the Spirit's relationship to Saul was conditional on his obedience in his role as Jehovah's anointed king. The Spirit's departure did not remove an inner saving experience; rather, it removed the divine enabling and approval needed for the kingship.

When David was chosen to replace Saul, we read, "Then Samuel took the horn of oil and anointed him in the midst of his brothers; and the Spirit of Jehovah came mightily upon David from that day forward" (1 Samuel 16:13). The Spirit's coming upon David marked him out as Jehovah's chosen king and equipped him for the difficult path ahead.

David's relationship to the Spirit appears again in his great penitential psalm after his sin with Bathsheba. In Psalm 51:11 he prays, "Do not cast me away from your presence and do not take your holy spirit from me." David had seen the Spirit depart from Saul and understood that his own sin deserved rejection. He pleads that Jehovah not remove that royal enabling of the Spirit.

David's words also show that he understood the Spirit's presence as precious and vulnerable to grieving. Yet even here the focus is not on an inward, general indwelling shared by all believers, but on the Spirit's presence with him in his unique role as king and psalmist.

The Spirit of God and Skilled Service

The Spirit's work was not limited to prophets and kings. Exodus 31:2–5 describes Bezalel, the chief craftsman of the tabernacle: Jehovah says, "I have filled him with the Spirit of God in wisdom, in understanding, in knowledge, and in all kinds of craftsmanship."

Here the Spirit equips a man for artistic and technical skill. Wisdom and understanding are not only moral or doctrinal but practical, enabling Bezalel to construct the tabernacle according to the pattern God revealed to Moses.

This shows that the Spirit of God empowers service in many forms, not only in preaching or ruling. When God has a work to be done according to His will, His Spirit equips the chosen worker to do it.

The Spirit and Prophetic Revelation

The Spirit as the Source of Prophecy

The clearest and most repeated Old Testament connection to the Spirit is in the realm of prophecy. The prophets did not speak from their own insight, imagination, or religious feeling; they spoke as the Spirit of God moved them.

The New Testament summarizes this when it says, "no prophecy was ever brought by the will of man, but men spoke from God as they were moved by the Holy Spirit" (2 Peter 1:21). That statement describes what was already true in the Old Testament: the Spirit of God is the divine author behind the prophetic word.

Old Testament writers testify to this repeatedly.

Nehemiah 9:30, reflecting on Israel's history, says, "You admonished them by your Spirit through your prophets, yet they would not give ear." God's Spirit was the One pleading with Israel through Isaiah, Jeremiah, Hosea, and the others. When they spoke, the Spirit spoke.

Ezekiel repeatedly hears God say, "The Spirit entered into me and set me on my feet, and he spoke with me." The prophets experience the Spirit as the One who gives them visions, understanding, and powerful words.

Micah 3:8 contrasts false prophets with himself and says, "But as for me, I am filled with power, with the Spirit of Jehovah, and with justice and might, to declare to Jacob his transgression and to Israel his sin." Here the prophet's courage and clarity come from the Spirit's empowering.

Zechariah 7:12 describes Israel's stubborn refusal to hear: "They made their hearts like flint so that they could not hear the law and the words which Jehovah of hosts had sent by his Spirit through the former prophets." Again, the Spirit is the One who sent the words.

From these passages we see that the Old Testament clearly teaches:
The Spirit of God is the true source of prophetic revelation. The prophets are human instruments; the Spirit is the divine Author.

The Spirit and Messianic Prophecy

Many of the most important Old Testament texts about the Spirit are directly tied to the coming Messiah. These texts show that the Spirit's work in the Old Testament was not an end in itself but a preparation for the coming of Christ and the new covenant.

Isaiah 11:1–2 promises, "Then a shoot will spring from the stem of Jesse, and a branch from his roots will bear fruit. The Spirit of Jehovah will rest on him, the spirit of wisdom and understanding, the spirit of counsel and might, the spirit of knowledge and the fear of Jehovah."

This prophecy describes a future descendant of David (the "stem of Jesse") upon whom the Spirit would rest in a permanent, complete way. Unlike Saul, from whom the Spirit departed, this future King would possess the Spirit in fullness, with wisdom, understanding, counsel, might, knowledge, and fear of Jehovah.

Isaiah 42:1 speaks of Jehovah's Servant: "Behold, my servant, whom I uphold; my chosen one in whom my soul delights. I have put my Spirit upon him; he will bring forth justice to the nations." This Servant is upheld and delighted in by Jehovah, and the Spirit is the One who equips Him to bring justice.

Isaiah 61:1–2 records the Messianic declaration that Jesus Himself would later read in the synagogue: "The Spirit of the Lord Jehovah is upon me, because Jehovah has anointed me to bring good news to the poor; he has sent me to bind up the brokenhearted, to proclaim liberty to captives and freedom to prisoners." Jesus applies this to Himself in Luke 4:18–21, making it clear that these Spirit-promises reach their fulfillment in His own ministry.

These passages show that the Old Testament Spirit-work is heading toward a goal: a Spirit-anointed Messiah who would preach good news, bring justice, and inaugurate a new era for God's people.

The Spirit as Holy and Good

Rare Old Testament Use of "Holy Spirit"

The exact phrase "Holy Spirit" appears only a few times in the Hebrew Old Testament, yet each appearance is significant.

Psalm 51:11 records David's plea, "Do not cast me away from your presence and do not take your holy spirit from me." Here "holy spirit" emphasizes the separateness and purity of God's empowering presence with David as king. His fear is that, because of his grievous sin, Jehovah would do with him what He had done with Saul and withdraw the Spirit's empowering favor.

Isaiah 63:10–11 speaks of Israel in the wilderness: "But they rebelled and grieved his holy Spirit; therefore he turned to be their enemy and he himself fought against them. Then his people remembered the days of old, of Moses: Where is he who brought them up out of the sea with the shepherds of his flock? Where is he who put his holy Spirit in the midst of them?"

Here, the people's rebellion is described as grieving God's holy Spirit. The Spirit had been "in the midst of them," meaning His presence was with the nation in a special way as He led them by the pillar of cloud and fire, empowered Moses, and guided them by revelation. Their sin provoked Him and brought discipline.

These texts show that even though the title "Holy Spirit" is rare, the Old Testament does describe the Spirit as holy, personal, and morally concerned. He can be grieved; He can withdraw His special presence; He can turn from favor to discipline when His holiness is despised.

"Your Good Spirit"

In addition to "holy spirit," the Old Testament also calls Him "your good Spirit."

Nehemiah 9:20, recounting the wilderness period, says of Jehovah, "You gave your good Spirit to instruct them." The Spirit is called "good" in relation to His instructing work. He is the One who gives guidance that is morally upright, beneficial, and consistent with God's covenant.

Psalm 143:10 prays, "Teach me to do your will, for you are my God; your Spirit is good; lead me in the land of uprightness" (UASV). Again, the Spirit is associated with teaching, leading, and uprightness.

In both cases, the Spirit is not only powerful but morally good and instructive. His goodness shows in the way He leads people into obedience and righteousness through God's revealed Word.

These expressions—"holy spirit" and "good Spirit"—underlined for Old Testament believers that the Spirit is not an impersonal energy. He is God's holy, good, personal power acting in history and in the midst of His people.

The Spirit and Individual Believers Under the Old Covenant

One of the most important questions about the Spirit in the Old Testament is how He related to ordinary believers—not just to prophets, judges, and kings, but to everyday men and women who feared Jehovah and trusted His promises.

The Old Testament does not present the Spirit as personally indwelling every believer in the same way that many modern readers assume from certain New Testament passages. Rather, the Old Testament emphasizes three main realities for individual believers.

Edward D. Andrews

The Spirit Worked Through the Word

Whenever the Spirit admonished, warned, comforted, or instructed Israel, He did so by means of the Word of God given through prophets, priests, and inspired writings.

As we saw, Nehemiah 9:30 says, "You admonished them by your Spirit through your prophets." The Spirit's tool was the prophetic message. His voice reached individual hearts when they heard and believed that Word.

This means that individual believers under the old covenant experienced the Spirit's work when they listened to and obeyed the revealed Word. Their hearts were stirred, conscience pricked, comfort given, and hope strengthened—not by a mystical inner whisper apart from the Word, but by the Spirit's power working through the Word.

The same pattern remains true today. The difference is not that the Spirit once used the Word but now bypasses it. The difference is that we now possess the complete Spirit-inspired Bible, Old and New Testaments, giving a fuller revelation of Christ and His saving work.

The Spirit Could Draw Near and Withdraw in Terms of Favor

Believers under the old covenant also knew that the Spirit of God could draw near in favor or withdraw in displeasure. This is why David prayed, "do not take your holy spirit from me." It is why Isaiah spoke of Israel grieving the holy Spirit in the wilderness and facing Jehovah as an enemy.

This drawing near and withdrawing does not describe a change in God's nature. Rather, it expresses a change in the way He deals with His people. When they trusted and obeyed, His Spirit was "in the midst of them" in blessing. When they rebelled, He withdrew that special blessing and brought discipline instead.

Old Testament believers were therefore deeply aware that the Spirit's favor must not be taken for granted. They knew that persistent rebellion could result in severe discipline and loss of the Spirit's empowering presence in their midst.

The Spirit Pointed Them Forward to a Greater Future

The prophets also promised that in the future, after the coming of the Messiah and the establishment of a new covenant, the Spirit's work among God's people would expand in a remarkable way.

Joel 2:28–29 says, "It will come about after this that I will pour out my Spirit on all flesh; and your sons and daughters will prophesy, your old men will dream dreams, your young men will see visions. Even on the male and female servants I will pour out my Spirit in those days."

This promise looks beyond the old covenant order. In the old covenant, prophets, kings, and certain leaders experienced a special coming of the Spirit. Joel speaks of a future "pouring out" on "all flesh"—that is, on all sorts of people among God's people—sons and daughters, old and young, servants and free.

Ezekiel 36:26–27 also promises, "I will give you a new heart and put a new spirit within you; and I will remove the heart of stone from your flesh and give you a heart of flesh. I will put my Spirit within you and cause you to walk in my statutes."

Here the promise of the Spirit is especially connected with inner renewal, a new heart, and empowered obedience. This description goes beyond what is typical in the old covenant experience and points forward to the blessings associated with Christ and the completed new covenant.

These promises do not contradict the Old Testament pattern; they show the direction in which that pattern was moving. The same Spirit who empowered judges and kings and inspired prophets would one day bring a deeper work of renewal through the full revelation of Christ and the completed inspired Scriptures.

Continuity and Discontinuity Between Old and New

To strengthen our understanding, we must hold together both the continuity and the change in the Spirit's work between the Old Testament and the New.

There is continuity. The same Spirit is at work in both Testaments. He is the Creator, the life-giver, the One who empowers servants of God, the Author of Scripture, and the One who confronts sin. He has always used the Word as His instrument when dealing with human hearts. He has always been holy and good, personal and active.

There is also discontinuity in emphasis and scope. Under the old covenant, the Spirit's special empowering and revelatory work was concentrated on a limited number of individuals—prophets, judges, kings, craftsmen, and elders. The average Israelite's direct experience of the Spirit was largely mediated through those Spirit-gifted leaders and through the Word they spoke and wrote.

Under the new covenant, especially in the apostolic age, the Spirit's special gifts were poured out more widely to establish the church and to complete the New Testament Scriptures. Those miraculous gifts have ceased with the passing of the apostles and the completion of the canon, but the Spirit continues to be present through His inspired Word, which remains fully sufficient for teaching, rebuking, correcting, and training in righteousness.

When we read the Old Testament with this understanding, we avoid two errors.

We do not flatten out the differences and pretend that Old Testament believers knew Christ and the Spirit in exactly the same way as first-century Christians. They did not have the full revelation of the cross, resurrection, and outpoured Spirit.

At the same time, we do not treat the Old Testament as if the Spirit were absent or inactive. He was profoundly active—in creation, in Israel's national life, in the prophetic word, and in the hearts of those who responded to that word in faith.

The Old Testament therefore gives us a rich, foundational picture of the Spirit of God: mighty in power, precise in purpose, holy in character, and always working through the revelation He Himself provides. That revelation leads us forward to the Messiah, Jesus Christ, upon whom the Spirit rested in fullness, and through whom the Spirit has given us the completed Scriptures that now guide the people of God until the return of Christ and the renewal of all things.

Edward D. Andrews

CHAPTER 2 The Person and the Divinity of the Holy Spirit

Many churchgoers are comfortable speaking about God the Father and Jesus Christ the Son as real Persons. Yet when the Holy Spirit is mentioned, the picture is often vague and hazy. Some think of the Spirit as a kind of spiritual electricity, a force or influence that comes from God but is not truly God. Others speak of the Spirit as "it" rather than "He," as if the Spirit were only an impersonal power. Still others react to excesses in modern charismatic movements by almost ignoring the Spirit altogether.

Scripture does not allow any of these mistakes. The Bible presents the Holy Spirit as a living, active, divine Person. He is not a "something"; He is a "Someone." He is not merely a power from God; He is Jehovah's own Spirit, fully sharing the divine nature, working in complete unity with the Father and the Son. At the same time, the Spirit is not a separate God. There is one God, Jehovah, known to us as Father, Son, and Holy Spirit.

In this chapter we will strengthen the case that the Holy Spirit is both personal and fully divine. We will show this from His actions, His characteristics, His relationships, His names, His attributes, and His works. We will also expose the serious errors that come from treating Him as an impersonal force.

The Question: Person or Impersonal Force?

Two broad views have appeared throughout church history. One claims that the Holy Spirit is nothing more than a divine influence, an impersonal power, or an emanation from Jehovah. In this view He is like light from the sun or electricity in a wire—real, powerful, but not personal. Some religious groups today openly teach this, reducing the Spirit to a kind of divine energy.

The other view, grounded solidly in Scripture, understands the Holy Spirit as a distinct Person within the one Godhead. He is not the Father, and He is not the Son, yet He is fully and truly God. He has a mind, a will, love, holiness, and the ability to speak, command, comfort, and grieve. This is the view consistently reflected in the New Testament and assumed by the writers of the Old.

Our task is not to build this doctrine from human philosophy, but to trace patiently what the Bible actually says and to let Scripture itself settle the matter.

Edward D. Andrews

How Scripture Speaks About the Spirit

The way the Bible talks about the Holy Spirit already points toward personality. Jesus did not describe the Spirit as "it," but as "another Helper." In the Upper Room, on the night before His execution, Jesus promised the apostles, "I will ask the Father, and He will give you another Helper, that He may be with you forever, the Spirit of truth" (John 14:16–17).

The word "another" shows that the Spirit is like Jesus in kind. Jesus Himself is clearly a Person; therefore, "another Helper" of the same kind must also be a Person. The title "Helper" (often translated "Comforter" or "Advocate") refers to someone who comes alongside to support, guide, and speak on behalf of another. This description does not fit a mere force.

Throughout John chapters 14–16, Jesus refers to the Spirit with personal pronouns and speaks of Him performing personal actions: teaching, reminding, testifying, guiding, hearing, speaking, and glorifying Christ. In everyday language, we instinctively use "he" or "she" for persons and "it" for things. Scripture follows this ordinary pattern when describing the Holy Spirit's work.

In the book of Acts the Spirit is described as speaking and issuing commands. "While they were ministering to Jehovah and fasting, the Holy Spirit said, 'Set apart for me Barnabas and Saul for the work to which I have called them'" (Acts 13:2). A mere impersonal energy does not speak in this way, does not call individuals, and does not use the language of "I" and "Me."

The consistent, natural language of Scripture talks about the Holy Spirit as "He," not "it," and presents Him as someone who communicates, thinks, decides, and responds. This is exactly how Scripture speaks when it is describing a Person.

The Spirit's Personal Actions

One of the simplest ways to see that the Holy Spirit is a Person is to notice what He does. The Bible attributes to the Spirit a series of actions that cannot be carried out by an impersonal power.

The Spirit speaks. Paul warns Timothy, "But the Spirit says expressly that in later times some will fall away from the faith" (1 Timothy 4:1). This is not a general feeling; it is a clear, specific message. An influence does not "say" anything.

The Spirit bears witness. Jesus says of Him, "When the Helper comes, whom I will send to you from the Father, the Spirit of truth who proceeds from the Father, He will bear witness about Me" (John 15:26). To bear witness is to testify, to present truth, to stand in court, as it were, and tell what is so. This again requires personhood.

The Spirit teaches and reminds. "But the Helper, the Holy Spirit, whom the Father will send in my name, that one will teach you all things and bring to your remembrance all that I have said to you." (John 14:26) Teaching is not merely transmitting power; it is communicating meaning, explaining, correcting, and reminding.

The Spirit guides into truth. Jesus says, "When he, the Spirit of truth, comes, he will guide you into all the truth" (John 16:13). Guiding involves intentional direction, choosing the path, and leading others onto that path.

The Spirit commands and forbids. In Acts 16:6–7 we read that Paul and his companions were "forbidden by the Holy Spirit to speak the word in Asia," and when they attempted to go into Bithynia, "the Spirit of Jesus did not allow them." A force does not forbid or allow in this personal way. Here, the Spirit exercises authority, directing where the gospel should and should not be preached at that moment.

The Spirit searches and knows. Paul writes, "God revealed them through the Spirit; for the Spirit searches all things, even the deep things of God" (1 Corinthians 2:10). Searching and examining the deep things of God and then revealing them to others is the work of a conscious, intelligent Person.

The Spirit intercedes. Romans 8:26–27 explains that in the weakness of believers, "the Spirit himself intercedes for us with groanings too deep for words... because he intercedes for the holy ones according to the will of God." Interceding means pleading on behalf of someone else. This is personal action at the highest level.

All of these verbs—speaks, testifies, teaches, guides, forbids, searches, intercedes—are personal verbs. They show will, intention, understanding, and relationship. Scripture never ascribes such actions to an impersonal force.

The Spirit's Personal Characteristics

Scripture not only describes the Spirit performing personal actions; it also ascribes to Him the inner qualities of a Person.

The Holy Spirit has a mind. Paul writes in Romans 8:27, "He who searches the hearts knows what the mind of the Spirit is, because he intercedes for the holy ones according to God." The word "mind" speaks of thought, intention, and understanding. The Spirit does not function blindly; He acts according to a wise plan.

The Holy Spirit possesses knowledge. In 1 Corinthians 2:11 Paul reasons, "For who among men knows the things of a man except the spirit of the man which is in him? Even so the things of God no one knows except the Spirit of God." The Spirit knows the things of God in a way parallel to how a human spirit knows the inner life of that person. The comparison assumes that the Spirit has conscious knowledge.

The Holy Spirit shows love. Paul appeals to the Roman congregation, "I urge you, brothers, through our Lord Jesus Christ and through the love of the Spirit, to strive together with me in your prayers to God for me" (Romans 15:30). Love is not an impersonal quality; it is a disposition of one person toward another. The Spirit's love is the ground of Paul's appeal.

The Holy Spirit has a will. In 1 Corinthians 12 Paul teaches about spiritual gifts and says that "one and the same Spirit works all these things, distributing to each one individually just as He wills" (1 Corinthians 12:11). The Spirit decides which gifts to give, to whom, and in what measure. This is a deliberate choice, not a mechanical process.

The Holy Spirit is good. Nehemiah looks back on Israel's history and says to God, "You gave your good Spirit to instruct them" (Nehemiah 9:20). Psalm 143:10 likewise prays, "Teach me to do Your will, for You are my God; Your Spirit is good; lead me in the land of uprightness." Goodness here is a moral quality, not merely a useful function. The Spirit is good in character, leading God's people into uprightness.

Mind, knowledge, love, will, and goodness—these are the essential marks of personhood. Scripture freely applies all of them to the Holy Spirit.

The Spirit's Personal Reactions to Human Beings

A further line of evidence for the Spirit's personality is the way He responds to people. The Bible describes the Spirit as being grieved, resisted, insulted, and lied to. None of this makes sense if He is only an impersonal energy.

The Spirit can be grieved. Paul commands believers, "Do not grieve the Holy Spirit of God, by whom you were sealed for the day of redemption" (Ephesians 4:30). Isaiah 63:10, speaking of Israel in the wilderness, says, "They rebelled and grieved His Holy Spirit; therefore He turned to be their enemy; He Himself fought against them." Grief is the pain of offended love and holiness. Only a Person can be grieved in this way.

The Spirit can be resisted. Stephen confronts the Sanhedrin and says, "You stiff-necked and uncircumcised in hearts and ears, you always resist the Holy Spirit" (Acts 7:51). To resist someone is to oppose His will, to refuse His instruction. Israel was not resisting an impersonal influence but the Spirit Himself.

The Spirit can be insulted and outraged. Hebrews 10:29 warns of severe judgment on the one who has "insulted the Spirit of grace." This is deeply personal language. An impersonal power cannot be insulted; only a Person can be treated with insolence and contempt.

The Spirit can be blasphemed. Jesus says that every sin and blasphemy will be forgiven people, "but the blasphemy against the Spirit will not be forgiven" (Matthew 12:31–32). Blasphemy is deliberate, slanderous speech against God. That this can be directed against the Holy Spirit shows that He is a divine Person, personally addressed and personally defamed.

The Spirit can be lied to. When Ananias and Sapphira secretly held back part of the proceeds from the sale of their land while pretending to give everything, Peter confronted Ananias: "Why has Satan filled your heart to lie to the Holy Spirit?" (Acts 5:3). One cannot lie to electricity or to a "force." One can lie only to a Person.

These texts form a consistent, cumulative picture. The Holy Spirit is not a faceless power. He is Jehovah's holy, good, personal Spirit, with whom human beings are in real relationship—either a relationship of obedience and reverence or one of rebellion and grief.

The Spirit in Relation to the Father and the Son

The Holy Spirit's personhood is also seen in His relationship to the Father and the Son. Scripture regularly speaks of the Spirit alongside the Father and the Son in ways that only make sense if all three are distinct Persons sharing the one divine nature.

At Jesus' baptism we see Father, Son, and Spirit active together. The Son is baptized in the Jordan, the Spirit descends upon Him like a dove, and the Father's voice from heaven declares, "You are my beloved Son; with you I am well pleased" (Mark 1:10–11). The Spirit is not the same Person as the Father, for the Father speaks from heaven while the Spirit descends upon the Son.

In the Great Commission Jesus commands, "Go therefore and make disciples of all the nations, baptizing them in the name of the Father and of the Son and of the Holy Spirit" (Matthew 28:19). There is one "name" but three distinct designations: Father, Son, and Holy Spirit. The Spirit is placed on the same level as the Father and the Son in the most solemn act of Christian initiation. It would be unthinkable to include a mere creature or a mere power in such a formula.

Paul's closing blessing to the Corinthian congregation provides a similar triadic pattern: "The grace of the Lord Jesus Christ, and the love of God, and the fellowship of the Holy Spirit be with you all" (2 Corinthians 13:14). The Holy Spirit is personally associated with "fellowship" in the same way that the Father is associated with love and the Son with grace.

Jesus speaks of the Spirit as "another Helper" whom the Father will send in the Son's name (John 14:16, 26). The Spirit "proceeds from the Father" and is sent by the Son (John 15:26). These expressions of sending and proceeding are relational. They show distinction without inequality. The Spirit is not simply the Father under another name; He is the Spirit of the Father and of the Son, united with Them, yet personally distinct.

When we put these passages together, we see that the Bible does not present a vague "three sides of God" or shifting roles of one Person, but a real, personal relationship between Father, Son, and Holy Spirit. The Spirit is fully involved in the work of revelation, redemption, and sanctification, alongside the Father and the Son.

The Deity of the Holy Spirit: His Names

Having seen that the Holy Spirit is a Person, we must also demonstrate that He is fully God. The Bible does this first through the names and titles given to Him.

He is called the "Spirit of God" and the "Spirit of Jehovah." These titles appear repeatedly in both Old and New Testaments. In the Old Testament, "the Spirit of God" moved over the waters at creation and came upon judges, kings, and prophets. In the New Testament, Paul writes of "the Spirit of God" dwelling in believers and calls Him "the Spirit of him who raised Jesus from the dead" (Romans 8:9, 11).

To speak of the "Spirit of God" does not mean a power separate from God. It means God's own Spirit, distinct in Person yet fully sharing the divine nature. When Scripture says "the Spirit of Jehovah," it does not describe something less than Jehovah, but Jehovah's own active presence and power.

He is called the "Holy Spirit." The word "holy" sets Him apart from all that is common or unclean. Holiness is one of the central attributes of God Himself. To call Him "the Holy Spirit" is to recognize that He is personally holy in the same way God is holy. This is not merely a description of His work; it is a title that belongs to Him as God's Spirit.

He is called "the Spirit of Christ" (Romans 8:9, 1 Peter 1:11), "the Spirit of his Son" (Galatians 4:6), and "the Spirit of Jesus" (Acts 16:7). These titles show the closest possible connection between the Spirit and Christ's own person and work. Christ is fully divine; His Spirit shares that same divine nature.

In Hebrews 10:15–17 the writer introduces a Scripture quotation by saying, "The Holy Spirit also testifies to us," and then cites words from Jeremiah, where Jehovah Himself is speaking. The Holy Spirit is identified with Jehovah's speaking voice.

In Acts 5:3–4, Peter first asks Ananias why he has lied to the Holy Spirit, and then says, "You have not lied to men but to God." To lie to the Holy Spirit is to lie to God. This is not a loose association; it is direct identification. The Spirit is God.

These names and identifications show that Scripture treats the Holy Spirit as no less divine than the Father and the Son.

The Deity of the Holy Spirit: His Attributes

The Holy Spirit also possesses divine attributes that belong to God alone.

The Spirit is eternal. Hebrews 9:14 describes Christ offering Himself "through the eternal Spirit." Eternity is a divine attribute. Created beings have a beginning; only God is truly eternal, without origin or ending. The Spirit is not brought into existence at some point; He is eternal Spirit.

The Spirit is omniscient. As we have seen, 1 Corinthians 2:10–11 says that the Spirit "searches all things, even the deep things of God," and that "no one knows the things of God except the Spirit of God." No creature, however exalted, can fully know the thoughts of God. For the Spirit to know all that God knows, He must Himself be God.

The Spirit is omnipresent. David asks, "Where can I go from Your Spirit? Or where can I flee from Your presence?" (Psalm 139:7). He then describes ascending to heaven or descending to the depths, and in every place Jehovah is present. The Spirit is everywhere present because He is Jehovah's own presence. Jeremiah 23:24 records Jehovah asking, "Do I not fill the heavens and the earth?." The Spirit shares this divine omnipresence.

The Spirit is omnipotent in the sense of exercising God's power. Micah says, "But as for me, I am filled with power—with the Spirit of Jehovah—and with justice and might, to declare to Jacob his transgression and to Israel his sin" (Micah 3:8). The Spirit empowers Micah with divine strength to speak boldly. The angel tells Mary that the Holy Spirit will come upon her and the power of the Most High will overshadow her, resulting in the conception of Jesus (Luke 1:35). Such acts require the full power of God.

Eternity, omniscience, omnipresence, and omnipotence are not qualities of a creature. They belong uniquely to God. When Scripture attributes them to the Holy Spirit, it declares His full deity.

The Deity of the Holy Spirit: His Works

The Bible also reveals the Spirit's deity through the works He performs—works that only God can do.

The Spirit is active in creation. Genesis 1:2 shows "the Spirit of God" moving over the waters at the dawn of creation. Job 26:13 states, "By His Spirit the heavens are made beautiful." Job 33:4 says, "The Spirit of God has made me, and the breath of the Almighty gives me life." Psalm 33:6 adds, "By the word of Jehovah the heavens were made, and by the breath of His mouth all their host." Creation is the work of God alone. Since the Spirit is Creator with the Father and the Son, He is fully divine.

The Spirit sustains and renews creation. Psalm 104:30 says to Jehovah, "You send forth Your Spirit, they are created; and You renew the face of the ground." The continued existence of living things depends on the Spirit's ongoing work.

The Spirit is the Author of Scripture. The Old Testament prophets spoke "by the Spirit of Jehovah," and the New Testament writers say that "no prophecy was ever brought by the will of man, but men spoke from God as they were moved by the Holy Spirit" (2 Peter 1:21). The words of Scripture are not merely religious reflections; they are the very words of God given through the Spirit. To be the divine Author of Scripture is to possess full deity.

The Spirit is involved in the new birth and new life. Jesus tells Nicodemus that no one can enter the kingdom of God unless he is born "of water and the Spirit" (John 3:5). This new birth is not a mystical feeling but the result of the Spirit's work through the Word of God, cleansing and renewing the heart. Titus 3:5 speaks of "the washing of regeneration and renewing by the Holy Spirit." The Spirit is the One who brings spiritual life where there was only death. Only God can give such life.

The Spirit is involved in resurrection. Romans 8:11 says, "If the Spirit of him who raised Jesus from the dead dwells in you, he who raised Christ Jesus from the dead will also give life to your mortal bodies through his Spirit who dwells in you."[1] The resurrection of Jesus is the decisive act of God's power. The Spirit is directly involved in that act and will be involved in the resurrection of believers as well.

---

[1] Romans 8:11 does not teach a literal, personal indwelling of the Holy Spirit within the bodies of believers; rather, Paul employs relational and representational language to describe the believer's new standing before God and the certainty of future resurrection. The expression "the Spirit of him who raised Jesus from the dead dwells in you" must be understood within the broader context of Romans 8, where Paul contrasts the mindset of the flesh with the mindset shaped by the Spirit's revealed Word (Romans 8:5–8). Paul's point is not that the Holy Spirit takes up residence inside Christians in a mystical or metaphysical sense, but that believers live under the rule, authority, and influence of the Spirit's teachings as revealed through Scripture. The same Spirit who raised Jesus from the dead guarantees the resurrection of the faithful by means of Jehovah's promise, not by an internal presence inside their mortal bodies. Paul frequently uses "in you" or "in us" language metaphorically to describe the governing authority of the gospel message (e.g., 1 Thessalonians 2:13; Colossians 3:16), not a literal indwelling of a divine Person. Within the grammatical-historical framework, "dwells" reflects covenantal relationship and indicative assurance, not spatial occupation. Furthermore, Paul's argument centers on future resurrection—Jehovah will "give life to your mortal bodies"—which is accomplished by divine power at the last day, not by an indwelling Spirit working internally throughout a believer's earthly life. To interpret Romans 8:11 as teaching a literal indwelling creates contradictions with other clear teachings of Scripture that root the Spirit's work exclusively in the inspired Word (John 17:17; 2 Timothy 3:16–17). Therefore, Romans 8:11 affirms resurrection certainty through the Spirit's past work in raising Jesus and the present authority of the Spirit-inspired Word, not a mystical indwelling of the Spirit in the Christian.

The Spirit is the source of genuine miracles. Jesus cast out demons "by the Spirit of God" (Matthew 12:28). In the apostolic era, healings, tongues, prophecies, and other miraculous gifts were given by the one Spirit, "who apportions to each one individually as He wills" (1 Corinthians 12:11). These signs were never random displays but targeted acts of God's power, carried out through the Spirit to confirm revelation and establish the early church.

Creation, inspiration of Scripture, new birth, resurrection, and miracles—these are uniquely divine works. Because the Spirit performs them, He is clearly shown to be God.

Avoiding Two Opposite Errors

Recognizing the Spirit as both Person and God guards us against two destructive errors.

The first error is reducing the Holy Spirit to an impersonal power. This empties the Bible's language of its meaning and turns a living relationship into a vague experience. If the Spirit is only a force, He cannot love, He cannot speak, He cannot be grieved, and He cannot comfort. Prayer, obedience, and reverence toward Him make no sense. Those who treat the Spirit as an "it" inevitably slide into ignoring Him or manipulating Him as if He were a power to be tapped into.

The second error is separating the Spirit from the Father and the Son in a way that undermines the unity of God. Scripture never invites us to think of three gods, or to approach the Spirit as if He were detached from Christ and the Father. The Spirit is always the Spirit of God and of Christ. He glorifies the Son and applies the work of the Father and the Son to human hearts through the Word.

Believers must hold these truths together. The Holy Spirit is a distinct, divine Person. He is not the Father and He is not the Son, yet

He is one with Them in nature, purpose, and work. He is Jehovah's own Spirit. To lie to Him is to lie to God. To resist Him is to resist God. To hear His voice in the Scriptures is to hear God Himself speaking.

The Personal and Divine Spirit in the Life of the Church

Understanding that the Spirit is both personal and divine also shapes how we think about His work today. The same Spirit who spoke through the prophets and apostles continues to speak through the completed, inspired Scriptures. He does not speak through new revelations that add to the Bible, nor does He bypass the Word with private inner messages. Instead, He applies the Word He inspired to hearts and minds, convincing, correcting, and comforting.

When believers open Scripture with reverent faith, the Holy Spirit is personally active. He illuminates the text, not by giving secret meanings, but by enabling clear understanding and a submissive heart. He presses home the reality of sin, the sufficiency of Christ, and the call to obedience. He stirs love, joy, peace, patience, kindness, goodness, faithfulness, gentleness, and self-control as the fruit of the Word believed and obeyed.

Because the Spirit is God, His work through the Word is powerful and effective. Because He is a Person, He can be trusted, loved, obeyed, and feared. The church does not live by human wisdom or human strength, but by the ongoing ministry of this personal, divine Spirit working through the inspired Scriptures He has given.

To confess the Holy Spirit as Person and as God, then, is not a speculative exercise. It is an essential part of biblical faith. It anchors our understanding of how God has spoken, how God saves, and how

God leads His people until the return of Christ. The Spirit of Jehovah, the Spirit of Christ, the Holy Spirit—He is the living God present and active through His Word, worthy of our honor, obedience, and grateful trust.

Edward D. Andrews

CHAPTER 3 The Holy Spirit and John the Baptist

When the New Testament opens, four centuries of prophetic silence are suddenly broken by a man standing in the wilderness, clothed in rough camel's hair, calling Israel to repent. That man is John the Baptist. He does not appear out of nowhere. His coming was predicted by the prophets, prepared by divine intervention in his parents' lives, and marked from the beginning by the special activity of the Holy Spirit.

John is a bridge between the old covenant and the new. He stands at the end of the line of Old Testament prophets and at the threshold of the ministry of Jesus Christ. Because of that, his relationship to the Holy Spirit is unique. He is filled with the Holy Spirit from his mother's womb. He preaches by the power of the Spirit. He identifies the Messiah on whom the Spirit descends and remains. And he announces a future baptism in the Holy Spirit and fire that would shape the entire apostolic age.

This chapter will explore these themes in depth. We will see how the Gospels present John's conception and birth as Spirit-guided, how his growth and character reflect the Spirit's work, how his preaching and baptismal ministry are tied directly to the Spirit, and how his words about baptism "in the Holy Spirit and fire" have often been misunderstood. Our aim is to show, carefully and exhaustively, what Scripture actually teaches and what it does not teach about the Holy Spirit in connection with John the Baptist.

The Spirit and the Birth of John

The first explicit reference to the Holy Spirit in the New Testament is linked to John's conception. Luke begins by introducing Zechariah and Elizabeth, a godly couple who "were both righteous in the sight of God, walking blamelessly in all the commandments and requirements of Jehovah," yet were childless and advanced in years. Their situation resembles several Old Testament couples (Abraham and Sarah, Elkanah and Hannah) through whom God brought about significant events in salvation history.

While Zechariah is serving in the temple, an angel of Jehovah appears and announces that his prayer has been heard: Elizabeth will bear a son and they are to call his name John. Several specific statements highlight the Holy Spirit's role. The angel says that John "will be great before Jehovah" and that "he will be filled with the Holy Spirit, even from his mother's womb." This is remarkable language.

First, being "filled with the Holy Spirit from the womb" shows that John's entire life and mission are Spirit-governed from the outset. He does not gradually grow into a prophetic calling on his own. His very existence and character are shaped by a special, sovereign work of the Spirit for a special purpose.

Second, this description sets John apart from ordinary believers. Scripture never presents every Israelite, or even every faithful believer, as filled with the Holy Spirit from the womb. John's experience is presented as unique because his task is unique: he will prepare the way for Jehovah's Messiah.

Third, this filling is connected with his Nazirite-like lifestyle: he is not to drink wine or strong drink. The angel's words echo Old Testament Nazirites, who were set apart in a special way for God's service. In John's case, the consecration is lifelong and deeper, tied directly to the Spirit's presence and his prophetic mission.

Luke further notes that when Mary visits Elizabeth, the baby in Elizabeth's womb leaps for joy and Elizabeth herself is filled with the Holy Spirit and speaks words of blessing. Later, when John is born and the people ask what this child will be, Zechariah is filled with the Holy Spirit and prophesies about the coming salvation in the Messiah and the role of his newborn son in that plan.

These scenes show the Holy Spirit as the active Author of this new stage in God's work. He shapes the womb, the child, the mother, and the father. He gives prophetic praise and interpretation, making it clear that John's birth is not a private family event but a turning point in redemptive history.

The Growth and Mission of John

Luke summarizes John's upbringing with simple but weighty words: "The child grew and became strong in spirit, and he lived in the desert until he appeared publicly to Israel." John does not grow up in the priestly routines of Jerusalem, even though his father is a priest. Instead, his life is marked by separation, simplicity, and spiritual strengthening.

"Became strong in spirit" does not refer to mystical experiences or dramatic emotions. It indicates a firm, resolute character shaped by the Spirit's work and grounded in the truth of God's Word. John's strength shows in his fearless preaching, his rejection of luxury, and his unshakable dedication to his calling even when that calling leads him to confront kings and eventually to imprisonment and death.

John's mission had already been described centuries earlier by the Holy Spirit speaking through the prophets. Isaiah records, "A voice of one calling out, 'In the wilderness, prepare the way of Jehovah; make straight in the desert a highway for our God. Every valley shall be lifted up, and every mountain and hill be made low; the uneven ground shall become level, and the rough places a plain. And the glory of Jehovah shall be revealed, and all flesh shall see it together, for the mouth of Jehovah has spoken.'"

Malachi likewise speaks of a coming messenger: "Look! I am sending my messenger, and he will prepare a way before me. And suddenly the true Lord, whom you are seeking, will come to his temple; and the messenger of the covenant will come, in whom you take delight. Look, he will certainly come," says Jehovah of armies.

The Holy Spirit had therefore already defined John's mission long before his birth. He would be the "voice in the wilderness," calling Israel to prepare the way of Jehovah, leveling spiritual obstacles, and pointing directly to the Messiah. He would be the "messenger" who prepares the way before the true Lord's coming to His temple.

When John appears near the Jordan River preaching repentance, he is not starting a new, self-chosen ministry. He is stepping into a role the Spirit had scripted centuries earlier. His clothing, his location, his message, and even his refusal to perform signs are all in harmony with that prophetic design.

The Spirit and John's Prophetic Ministry

John begins preaching in the fifteenth year of Tiberius Caesar. His message is summarized as a "baptism of repentance for the forgiveness of sins." This does not mean that the physical act of being immersed in water itself washes away sin. Rather, his baptism is the God-given outward expression of genuine repentance. Those who heard his message, turned from their sins, and submitted to baptism were publicly declaring their readiness to welcome the coming Messiah.

John's preaching is marked by Spirit-given clarity and boldness. He speaks plainly to all classes of people. When crowds come, he addresses their hypocrisy and warns them not to rely on physical descent from Abraham. When tax collectors and soldiers ask what they should do, he gives practical, moral instructions. When religious leaders appear, he exposes their spiritual pride and calls them a brood of vipers.

This fearless proclamation resembles Old Testament prophets like Elijah and Amos, and that similarity is intentional. The Spirit shapes John's ministry as a prophetic call to repentance at the turning of the ages. He is not trying to be clever or innovative; he is delivering the message the Spirit has given.

John's central role, however, is not simply to persuade people to repent. His greatest task is to identify the Messiah. When Jesus approaches, John declares, "Look, the Lamb of God, who takes away the sin of the world!" He then explains that he himself did not know who the Messiah would be until a particular sign revealed Him: "I saw the Spirit descend from heaven like a dove, and it remained on him... the one who sent me to baptize in water said to me, 'The one on whom you see the Spirit descending and remaining on him, this is he who baptizes in the Holy Spirit.' I have seen and I have borne witness that this is the Son of God."

Again, the Holy Spirit stands at the center. The Father had told John that the visible descent of the Spirit would mark the Messiah. John's testimony about Jesus is therefore directly grounded in what the Spirit revealed and did. John does not choose Jesus as Messiah; he recognizes Him according to the Spirit's sign.

The Spirit and the Baptism of Jesus

The baptism of Jesus at the Jordan is one of the most important events in the Gospels, and John is the human instrument who performs it. All four Gospels record that when Jesus is baptized, the heavens open, the Spirit of God descends on Him like a dove, and a voice from heaven declares Him to be the beloved Son.

From John's perspective, this is the fulfillment of the sign he had been given. The Spirit's descent and remaining on Jesus confirms that this is the One who will baptize in the Holy Spirit. The symbolism of the dove draws attention to purity, gentleness, and the beginning of a new era, much as the dove signaled new conditions after the Flood in Noah's day.

Jesus does not receive the Spirit because He previously lacked holiness or needed moral improvement. He is already the sinless Son of God. The descent of the Spirit marks His public anointing for His ministry. Isaiah had promised that the Spirit of Jehovah would rest upon the Messiah in fullness—as the Spirit of wisdom, understanding, counsel, might, knowledge, and the fear of Jehovah. At the Jordan that promise is publicly displayed.

John's role is to witness this anointing and to testify to Israel that this Spirit-anointed Jesus is the long-promised Son of God, the Lamb of God, and the One who will bring about a new stage of the Spirit's work.

The Baptism of the Holy Spirit and Fire

The next major connection between John the Baptist and the Holy Spirit is his teaching about baptism "in the Holy Spirit and fire." This teaching is so important and so often misunderstood that it deserves careful, patient examination.

John distinguishes sharply between his baptism and that of the coming One. He says that he baptizes with water for repentance, but the Coming One, who is mightier than he and whose sandals he is unworthy to remove, will baptize with the Holy Spirit and fire. He adds imagery of judgment: the axe at the root of the trees, trees that do not bear good fruit being cut down and thrown into the fire, a winnowing fork in the Messiah's hand, wheat gathered into the barn, and chaff burned with unquenchable fire.

Several points must be established from the text itself.

First, John is speaking to a mixed crowd. Some hear his message humbly and submit to baptism. Others come out from curiosity or pride and refuse to repent. His words about trees and chaff clearly distinguish between those who will be saved and those who will face judgment.

Second, the immediate context closely associates "fire" with judgment, not with spiritual vitality. Trees that do not bear good fruit are cut down and thrown into the fire. Chaff is burned with unquenchable fire. Fire, in this context, is the destiny of the unrepentant.

Third, John uses two prepositional phrases—"with the Holy Spirit" and "with fire"—under one verb "he will baptize," but the imagery of trees and chaff makes it plain that he is describing two contrasting outcomes from the ministry of the Messiah. Those who receive Him will be immersed, as it were, in the Holy Spirit's power and blessing. Those who reject Him will be immersed in fiery judgment.

Many modern teachers merge these into a single experience and speak of a "baptism of the Holy Spirit and fire" that all believers should seek, often understood as a heightened emotional or charismatic experience. But to do that is to ignore how John himself explains the fire images immediately before and after the statement. Fire in this context does not signify a deeper blessing for the already saved, but the devastating end of the fruitless and the chaff.

If we take John's words in their own setting, therefore, we see that he is presenting both promise and warning. The Messiah will pour out the Holy Spirit in a new and powerful way on His people, and He will also bring the fire of judgment on those who refuse to repent.

The Fulfillment of Baptism in the Holy Spirit

If John's prediction about baptism in the Holy Spirit is real and literal, we should expect Scripture to show us its fulfillment. The book of Acts does exactly that.

Just before His ascension, Jesus tells the apostles that they will be "baptized with the Holy Spirit not many days from now." He connects this directly with the coming of power and the beginning of their worldwide witness. This clearly echoes John's prediction and locates its initial fulfillment at Pentecost.

On the day of Pentecost, the apostles are all together when a sound like a violent wind fills the house and tongues as of fire rest on each of them. They are filled with the Holy Spirit and begin to speak in other languages, declaring the mighty works of God. This event is not a private inner feeling; it is a public, miraculous, historical outpouring.

Peter explicitly ties what is happening to the prophetic promise of the Spirit and to the exaltation of Christ. He explains to the crowd that Jesus, having been raised and exalted to the right hand of God, has "poured out" what they see and hear. The language of "pouring out" echoes Joel's prophecy and matches John's picture of baptism in the Holy Spirit: an overwhelming, abundant giving of the Spirit's power to inaugurate a new era.

Later, when Peter preaches to Cornelius and his household, the Holy Spirit falls on them in a way that parallels Pentecost. They speak in other languages and magnify God. Peter and the Jewish believers recognize this as the same kind of event: "The Holy Spirit fell on them just as on us at the beginning." Peter recalls Jesus' words about being baptized with the Holy Spirit and concludes that God has given the same gift to Gentiles who believe.

From these passages we can see several important truths about Spirit baptism.

First, baptism in the Holy Spirit is a once-for-history kind of event tied to the transition from the old covenant to the new and to the inclusion of Gentiles. It is not repeatedly commanded or sought as an ongoing, private experience.

Second, the purpose of this baptism is not inner cleansing from sin—Christ's sacrifice and the application of His blood bring forgiveness—but empowerment and confirmation of the apostolic message. The Spirit's miraculous signs publicly authenticate that

Jesus is Lord and that Jews and Gentiles alike are included in the new covenant people through faith in Him.

Third, these events are exceptional in Scripture, not routine. The language of being "baptized with the Holy Spirit" appears only in connection with John's prediction, Jesus' promise just before Pentecost, and Peter's interpretation of Pentecost and Cornelius' experience. This concentration of references shows that Spirit baptism belongs to the foundational stage of the church, not to every believer's everyday experience.

Thus, when John identifies Jesus as the One who baptizes in the Holy Spirit, he is pointing to Christ's authority to pour out the Spirit in this epoch-making way to launch the apostolic church and to confirm the gospel to both Jews and Gentiles.

Clarifying What Baptism in the Holy Spirit Is Not

Because the phrase "baptism in the Holy Spirit" sounds powerful and attractive, it has often been misused. For the sake of clarity and faithfulness to Scripture, we must carefully state what it is not.

It is not a second blessing reserved for some Christians beyond ordinary conversion. The New Testament never commands believers to seek "Spirit baptism" as a later experience. Every believer receives the benefits of what Christ accomplished at Pentecost, but the historical event itself is not repeated.

It is not identical with receiving the Holy Spirit at conversion. When people obey the gospel today—believing in Christ, repenting, and being baptized in water in His name—they are forgiven and added to the body of Christ. The Spirit works through the gospel and through the written Word, but Scripture does not describe each new convert as being "baptized with the Holy Spirit" in the Pentecost sense.

It is not a guarantee of continuing miraculous gifts in the modern church. The apostolic era was marked by signs and wonders given by the Spirit to confirm the new revelation. Once the New Testament Scriptures were completed and the last apostle died, those signs ceased. We now have the permanent, Spirit-inspired Word of God as our authority and guidance, rather than ongoing miraculous confirmations.

It is not the same as the "baptism of fire." As we have already seen, the baptism of fire points to judgment on the unrepentant, not to a more intense blessing on the faithful. To pray for "fire" in this sense is to ask for something Scripture consistently portrays as destruction, not sanctification.

By removing these misconceptions, we preserve John's words in their intended force: a mighty promise of Christ's authority to pour out the Spirit in inaugurating the church, and a solemn warning that those who refuse the Messiah will face fiery judgment.

John the Baptist and the End of the Old Covenant Age

The Holy Spirit's role in John's life also teaches us how God orchestrates the turning points of history. John is more than a colorful preacher; he is the Spirit-empowered forerunner who marks the end of one order and the arrival of another.

Jesus Himself says that among those born of women, no one greater than John has arisen, yet the least in the kingdom of God is greater than he. This surprising statement shows that John belongs to the old covenant side of the line. He is the greatest representative of that older era, but he stands just short of the full realities of the kingdom that Jesus brings.

The Spirit filled John from the womb, strengthened him in the wilderness, guided his preaching, and enabled him to identify the Messiah. Yet John did not live to see Pentecost, the full outpouring of the Spirit, or the spread of the gospel to the nations. He announces these things; he does not personally experience them in the way later believers do.

This reinforces the fact that the Spirit's work is progressive across history. The same Holy Spirit who spoke through the prophets, filled John, descended on Jesus, and baptized the apostles into their Pentecost ministry is the One who later inspired the writing of the New Testament and continues to work through those Scriptures today. There is one Spirit, one plan, and one unfolding story.

For modern believers, John's Spirit-empowered ministry stands as both an encouragement and a warning. It encourages us because it shows that God is faithful to His promises. What the Spirit foretold through Isaiah and Malachi, He fulfilled exactly in John. What John preached about the coming Messiah and the Spirit's outpouring came to pass exactly as announced. We can therefore trust every word the Spirit has breathed into Scripture.

It warns us because the same message John proclaimed still applies. The Messiah has come, and the axe is still at the root of the trees. Fruitless religiosity will be cut down. The chaff will still be burned with unquenchable fire. To ignore the Spirit's witness to Christ in Scripture is to place oneself among those who face the baptism of fire rather than the blessing of the Spirit.

John the Baptist, then, is not a figure to be admired from a distance and then forgotten. His Spirit-shaped life and message still call out across the centuries: repent, turn to the Lamb of God, and receive the salvation He brings. The Holy Spirit who prepared John, empowered John, and confirmed John's testimony now speaks in the completed Word, pressing the same call upon every hearer.

CHAPTER 4 The Holy Spirit and Jesus

The relationship between the Holy Spirit and Jesus Christ stretches from eternity into history and then forward into our future hope. The Spirit does not appear alongside Jesus as an optional extra. From the first promises of a coming Messiah, to the virgin conception, to the public ministry of Jesus, to His sacrificial death, bodily resurrection, exaltation, and ongoing ministry from heaven, the Holy Spirit is constantly present, active, and essential.

When we carefully follow the biblical record using a historical-grammatical method, we see that the Spirit's activity in the life of Jesus is not vague or symbolic. It is specific, historical, and doctrinally rich. This chapter will show, with as much thorough biblical evidence as possible, that Jesus' entire mission—before He was born, during

His earthly ministry, in His death, and in His exaltation—is inseparably connected to the Holy Spirit.

By doing this, we also see how completely Jehovah has coordinated the work of the Son and the Spirit for our salvation. The Spirit glorifies the Son, the Son perfectly obeys the Father, and the unified work of the triune God stands at the heart of the Christian faith.

The Holy Spirit Foretells the Coming of Christ

Long before Jesus was born in Bethlehem, the Holy Spirit was already at work, speaking through the Hebrew prophets and setting the stage for His arrival. The New Testament explicitly states that prophecy is not human speculation, but the result of men being "carried along by the holy spirit" (2 Peter 1:21). The prophets, as Peter explains, searched and inquired about the salvation that was to come, as "the spirit of Christ" in them pointed ahead to His sufferings and the glories to follow (1 Peter 1:10–11).

So, when we talk about Old Testament prophecy regarding Christ, we are talking about the work of the Holy Spirit centuries before Bethlehem. The Spirit did not speak vaguely. He revealed the time period, the place, the lineage, and even key events of the Messiah's life, death, and exaltation.

The Time Frame of the Messiah's Coming

The old chapter mentioned Isaiah 2:2, which says,

It will come to pass in the latter days that the mountain of the house of Jehovah will be established on the top of the mountains, and will be lifted up above the hills; and all the nations will stream to it.

This prophecy describes a future period when the true worship of Jehovah, centered on His "house," would be elevated and nations would stream to it. The "latter days" language points to a decisive turning point in redemptive history, not an endless, undefined future. The Holy Spirit, through Isaiah, announces that Jehovah's saving rule will be openly revealed and that this revelation will draw the nations.

However, the Spirit gives even more precise markers through other prophets. Malachi 3:1 says,

Look! I am going to send my messenger, and he will prepare the way before me. And the Lord whom you are seeking will come suddenly to his temple, and the messenger of the covenant will come, in whom you take delight, behold, he is coming," says Jehovah of hosts.

This prophecy, given late in Old Testament history, states that "the Lord" whom Israel was seeking would come suddenly to "his temple." This is not a vague spiritual temple but the actual temple in Jerusalem that stood in Malachi's day—the Second Temple.

The implications are enormous. The Holy Spirit is telling us that the Messiah would appear while that temple still stood. Since that temple was destroyed by the Romans in 70 C.E., any claim that the Messiah has not yet come runs directly against Malachi's Spirit-inspired words. The Spirit binds Messiah's appearance to a definite historical window.

Haggai delivers a similar message. He speaks of the glory of the "latter house" (the Second Temple) surpassing that of Solomon's temple, and Jehovah promises, "in this place I will give peace" (Haggai 2:9). The greater glory of that temple is not in its architecture but in the presence of the Messiah Himself. When Jesus entered the temple, taught there, and cleansed it, the greater glory arrived. The Holy Spirit, through Haggai, pointed forward to that reality.

Daniel 2 and Daniel 9 further tighten the time frame. In Daniel 2, the kingdom of God is established "in the days of those kings," describing a sequence of empires that culminates in the Roman Empire. In Daniel 9:24–27, a specific period ("seventy weeks") is linked to the coming of "an anointed one, a prince" who would be "cut off." The details of that prophecy are complex, but the central point is clear: the Messiah must come, and be rejected, within a specific historical period before the destruction of Jerusalem and its sanctuary.

The Spirit, therefore, does not leave the timing of Messiah's coming open-ended. Jesus' birth, life, and death all occur in the exact historical window the Holy Spirit laid down centuries before: during the era of the Second Temple, under Roman rule, before the temple's destruction. This is powerful evidence that the coming of Jesus is the precise fulfillment of Spirit-given prophecy, not a convenient afterthought by the early church.

The Place and Lineage of His Birth

The Holy Spirit did not merely say that the Messiah would appear at a certain time. He also foretold the place and family line from which He would come.

Micah 5:2 says,

But you, Bethlehem Ephrathah, though you are little among the thousands of Judah, yet out of you shall come forth to me the one to be ruler in Israel, whose goings forth are from of old, from everlasting.

This prophecy narrows the birthplace of the Messiah to a small town, Bethlehem Ephrathah, in Judah. It further says that this ruler's "goings forth are from of old, from everlasting." The Holy Spirit points to a ruler who is both connected to Bethlehem in history and yet has a pre-temporal origin. This fits Jesus Christ and no one else.

The Jewish leaders at the time of Jesus also understood Micah 5:2 in a messianic way. When Herod asked where the Christ was to be born, the chief priests and scribes immediately cited this text and said He would be born in Bethlehem (Matthew 2:4–6). The understanding that the Messiah would come from Bethlehem did not originate with Christians; it was already the expectation among the Jews.

The Spirit also specifies the Messiah's broader family line. Jehovah tells Abraham,

I will bless those who bless you, and him who dishonors you I will curse, and in you all the families of the earth shall be blessed. (Genesis 12:3)

The promise is that the blessing for "all the families of the earth" would come through Abraham's line. Later passages narrow this further to Isaac, then to Jacob, and ultimately to the tribe of Judah (Genesis 49:10). Jehovah's covenant with David in 2 Samuel 7 establishes that an eternal ruler will come from David's house.

The New Testament confirms that Jesus belongs to Abraham's and David's line through carefully preserved genealogies (Matthew 1:1–17; Luke 3:23–38). Hebrews 2:16 underlines that He did not come to help angels but "the offspring of Abraham." The Spirit-given Old Testament promises require a Messiah from Abraham, from Judah, from David, and from Bethlehem. Jesus Christ alone fits all of these Spirit-defined criteria.

Furthermore, after 70 C.E. the genealogical records kept in the temple were destroyed. This means that today, no one can verifiably prove that he is a son of David in the precise way required of the Messiah. The Holy Spirit's prophetic markers—time, temple, lineage, place of birth—leave no open door for a still-future Messiah who is yet to be identified. The evidence points decisively to Jesus of Nazareth.

His Suffering, Betrayal, and Resurrection Foretold

The old chapter rightly pointed to several key texts. Psalm 41:9 says,

Even my close friend in whom I trusted, who ate my bread, has lifted his heel against me.

In its original setting, this is David speaking, but the Holy Spirit uses David's experience to speak prophetically of the Messiah as well. Jesus Himself applies this verse to His betrayal by Judas (John 13:18). This is not a random detail. The betrayal comes from someone who shared bread with Him, someone counted as a close companion.

Isaiah 53:7 describes the Servant of Jehovah:

He was oppressed, and he was afflicted, yet he opened not his mouth; like a lamb that is led to the slaughter, and like a sheep that before its shearers is silent, so he opened not his mouth.

This matches the New Testament picture of Jesus' behavior before the high priest, Herod, and Pilate. While He does speak, He refuses to answer in a way that defends Himself or avoids the path to the cross. He does not rage or threaten. His silence and submission fulfill the Spirit's earlier description of the suffering Servant.

Psalm 16:10 says,

For you will not abandon my soul to Sheol, or let your holy one see corruption.

Peter, in Acts 2, argues that David could not ultimately be talking about himself, because David died, was buried, and his tomb was still known in Jerusalem. The Spirit-inspired words point beyond

David to the Messiah, whose body would not decay in the grave. Jesus' resurrection on the third day, with an empty tomb and repeated appearances, fulfills the promise that Jehovah would not let His "holy one see corruption."

Daniel 7:13–14 shows the coronation side of the story:

I saw in the night visions, and behold, with the clouds of heaven there came one like a son of man, and he came to the Ancient of Days and was presented before him. And to him was given dominion and glory and a kingdom, that all peoples, nations, and languages should serve him; his dominion is an everlasting dominion, which shall not pass away, and his kingdom one that shall not be destroyed.

Here the "son of man" is brought before the Ancient of Days (Jehovah) and given everlasting dominion. The Holy Spirit inspired Daniel to record this heavenly scene centuries before Jesus. The New Testament links Jesus' ascension and exaltation to this text. The resurrection is not merely a return to life; it leads to enthronement at Jehovah's right hand over an everlasting kingdom.

All of this—betrayal, suffering, silent submission, resurrection, and exaltation—was clearly described beforehand by the Holy Spirit. These are not vague religious ideas. They are specific historical claims that fit Jesus Christ and no one else.

The Holy Spirit and the Incarnation of the Son

The Old Testament prophecies narrow our focus to a particular time, family line, and place. The New Testament then shows how the Holy Spirit brings the eternal Son into the world through the virgin conception. The Spirit is not merely a distant witness; He is the direct divine agent by whom the Son takes on human nature.

Matthew 1:18 records,

Now the birth of Jesus Christ took place in this way. When his mother Mary had been betrothed to Joseph, before they came together she was found to be with child from the Holy Spirit.

This short sentence denies any natural explanation. Mary and Joseph had not yet lived together as husband and wife, and yet Mary is pregnant. The explanation given is not rumor or speculation; it is the direct statement of inspired Scripture: she is "with child from the Holy Spirit."

Luke 1:35 adds more detail. The angel says to Mary,

The Holy Spirit will come upon you, and the power of the Most High will overshadow you; therefore the child to be born will be called holy—the Son of God.

The language here echoes Genesis 1:2, where the Spirit of God is described as hovering over the surface of the waters at creation. Just as the Spirit was present and active at the original creation, so He is now present and active in the new creation that begins with the incarnation. The "power of the Most High" overshadowing Mary is not a crude physical idea but a sacred, sovereign act of God bringing about conception without a human father.

The result is that Jesus is both fully human and uniquely "the Son of God." He is truly born of a woman, sharing our humanity, yet without inherited sin. At the same time, He does not come into existence in the womb; His "goings forth are from of old, from everlasting" as Micah 5:2 states. The Holy Spirit's action in the virgin conception is how the eternal Son takes on real human nature and enters history as the Messiah.

Some claim that the virgin birth is a later legend borrowed from pagan myths. This does not stand up to serious comparison. Pagan stories often involve crude unions between gods and women or fantastical scenarios that bear no resemblance to the sober, historically anchored accounts in Matthew and Luke. Moreover, the Jewish environment in which these Gospels were written was not friendly to pagan myths. The virgin conception of Jesus is presented as a factual, Spirit-wrought miracle, not a religious symbol.

Others suggest that Jesus only became the Son of God at His baptism, as if the Spirit's descent then "adopted" Him into divine status. This contradicts the clear testimony of the conception narratives. He is already "holy" and already "the Son of God" at conception. The baptism is His public anointing as Messiah, not His promotion into deity. The Holy Spirit makes sure that from the very beginning we know who this child is.

The Spirit's Anointing and Empowering of Jesus' Ministry

The title "Christ" means "anointed one." The Old Testament anticipates a figure anointed by the Spirit to bring justice, proclaim good news, and establish the rule of Jehovah. Isaiah 11:1–2 describes a shoot from the stump of Jesse on whom "the spirit of Jehovah" will rest. Isaiah 42:1 presents Jehovah's Servant, "my chosen, in whom my soul delights," and says, "I have put my spirit upon him." Isaiah 61:1 says, "The spirit of the Lord Jehovah is upon me, because Jehovah has anointed me to bring good news to the poor."

All of these Spirit-inspired prophecies converge on one person. When Jesus appears at the Jordan River, the Holy Spirit makes the identification unmistakable.

The Baptism and the Descent of the Spirit

Matthew 3:16–17 records,

And when Jesus was baptized, immediately he went up from the water, and behold, the heavens were opened to him, and he saw the

Spirit of God descending like a dove and coming to rest on him; and behold, a voice from heaven said, "This is my beloved Son, with whom I am well pleased."

Here we see Father, Son, and Spirit together in one scene. The Spirit descends and "comes to rest" on Jesus. The Father speaks words of approval and delight. Jesus, the incarnate Son, stands in the water in obedience. The anointing promised in Isaiah is now visible and public.

This does not mean that Jesus lacked the Spirit before this moment. As the eternal Son, He has always been in perfect fellowship with the Spirit. As the incarnate Son, conceived by the Holy Spirit, He has never been separated from the Spirit's presence. But at the baptism, the anointing is revealed and announced. It marks the formal beginning of His public ministry as the Christ.

Led by the Spirit into Confrontation with Satan

Immediately after the baptism, the Gospels tell us that Jesus was led by the Spirit into the wilderness. Matthew 4:1 says,

Then Jesus was led up by the Spirit into the wilderness to be tempted by the devil.

Mark emphasizes the intensity of this leading:

The Spirit immediately drove him out into the wilderness. (Mark 1:12)

Luke adds that Jesus was "full of the Holy Spirit" and that He was "led by the Spirit in the wilderness" (Luke 4:1).

The Holy Spirit is not absent when Jesus faces the devil. He is the One who leads Jesus into the conflict. This shows that the confrontation is part of the Father's plan, not a random attack. Jesus faces temptation not as an isolated individual but as the obedient Son, empowered and guided by the Spirit, standing where Adam failed and where Israel failed in their wilderness wanderings.

Notice how Jesus responds to each temptation. He does not appeal to private mystical experiences or feelings. He answers with "It is written," quoting Deuteronomy. The same Spirit who inspired those Scriptures now strengthens the incarnate Son to stand on them. The Spirit and the Word are never in competition. The Spirit uses the Word He has given.

For Christians, this is a vital pattern. If Jesus, the sinless Son of God, faced Satan armed with the written Word, we must never imagine that our fight against sin and deception can be waged by feelings or supposed inner voices. The Holy Spirit strengthens us through the Scriptures He has inspired. Jesus' obedience in the wilderness is both our salvation (because He succeeded where we have failed) and our model.

Miracles Performed by the Power of the Spirit

Jesus' miracles are not random displays of power. They are signs of the kingdom, acts of compassion, and demonstrations that the promised Spirit-anointed Messiah has arrived. The Holy Spirit is central to these works.

In Matthew 12, when Jesus casts out a demon from a man who was blind and mute, the crowds are astonished, but the Pharisees accuse Him of casting out demons by the power of Beelzebul. Jesus answers,

But if it is by the Spirit of God that I cast out demons, then the kingdom of God has come upon you. (Matthew 12:28)

Jesus explicitly states that His exorcisms are done "by the Spirit of God." This is crucial. He does not merely say that He casts out demons because He is powerful or because He is the Son. He points to the Spirit of God as the immediate agent. The conclusion He draws is that the arrival of the kingdom of God is evidenced by the Spirit's activity through Him.

This also explains why blasphemy against the Holy Spirit is so serious. When the religious leaders attribute the Spirit's work in Jesus to Satan, they are not just making a small mistake; they are willfully rejecting clear evidence that the Holy Spirit is bearing witness to the Messiah. To look at the Spirit's testimony to Christ and call it demonic is to harden oneself against the very means by which Jehovah calls people to repentance and faith.

The Gospels are filled with signs and wonders: healings, raising the dead, calming storms, feeding multitudes. These wonders are real historical events, not legends. They were not denied by Jesus' enemies; instead, His enemies tried to discredit the source of His power. The Holy Spirit empowers Jesus to perform these miracles as part of His messianic mission. They show His compassion, His authority, and the reality of the kingdom breaking into this fallen world.

Preaching and Joy in the Holy Spirit

Jesus' ministry is also marked by Spirit-empowered preaching. In Luke 4, He reads from Isaiah 61 in the synagogue:

The spirit of the Lord is upon me, because he has anointed me to proclaim good news to the poor.

After reading, He says, "Today this Scripture has been fulfilled in your hearing" (Luke 4:21). He identifies Himself as the One anointed by the Spirit to proclaim the gospel. His teaching astonishes people because He speaks with authority, and that authority is linked to the Spirit of God resting upon Him.

Luke 10:21 describes a remarkable moment:

In that same hour he rejoiced in the holy spirit and said, "I thank you, Father, Lord of heaven and earth..."

Jesus rejoices "in the holy spirit" as He praises the Father for His sovereign work in revealing truth to the humble. The joy of the Son, the work of the Father, and the presence of the Holy Spirit are united. This again shows that the Spirit is actively involved in Jesus' inner life, His worship, and His communion with the Father.

The Holy Spirit and the Sacrifice of Christ

The climax of Jesus' earthly mission is His sacrificial death. The Holy Spirit does not step aside at this point. He is directly involved in the offering of the Son.

Hebrews 9:14 asks,

How much more will the blood of Christ, who through the eternal Spirit offered himself without blemish to God, purify our conscience from dead works to serve the living God.

This is one of the most profound statements about the cross in the New Testament. It tells us that Christ did not go to the cross as a helpless victim. He "offered himself" to God. The offering is voluntary and obedient. But He does so "through the eternal Spirit."

The phrase "eternal Spirit" highlights the deity of the Holy Spirit. He is not a created force. He is eternal, as only God is eternal. Through this eternal Spirit, Christ offers Himself "without blemish" to God. The Spirit, who had anointed Jesus for ministry and empowered Him in obedience, sustains Him as He bears our sins. The cross is the united work of the triune God: the Father purposes and receives the sacrifice, the Son offers Himself, and the Holy Spirit is the divine agent through whom that offering is made.

We have already seen that the Holy Spirit foretold the betrayal and silent submission of the Servant in passages like Psalm 41:9 and

Isaiah 53:7. The Gospels make clear that these events happen "that the Scriptures might be fulfilled." The Spirit does not predict one thing and then watch helplessly as events take another course. What He foretold, He also oversees and brings to pass according to the will of Jehovah.

In Gethsemane, Jesus prays with intense anguish, yet submits to the Father's will. Although the text does not explicitly mention the Holy Spirit there, we know from the broader teaching of Scripture that the Spirit is never absent from the Son's obedience. The same Spirit who strengthened Him in the wilderness now sustains Him in His deepest agony as He resolves to drink the cup given by the Father.

Understanding the Spirit's role in the sacrifice protects us from thinking of the cross as a tragic mistake, a mere victory of human evil, or something that caught God by surprise. The offering of Christ "through the eternal Spirit" shows that this is the center of Jehovah's saving plan, executed in perfect unity by the Father, the Son, and the Holy Spirit.

The Holy Spirit and the Resurrection, Exaltation, and Commission of Christ

The resurrection and exaltation of Jesus are also the work of the Holy Spirit. The Spirit who hovered over the primeval waters, who overshadowed Mary, who anointed and empowered Jesus' ministry, now acts in resurrection power.

Romans 8:11 says,

If the Spirit of him who raised Jesus from the dead dwells in you, he who raised Christ Jesus from the dead will also give life to your mortal bodies through his Spirit who dwells in you.

This verse attributes Jesus' resurrection to "the Spirit of him who raised Jesus from the dead." The Father raised the Son, and He did so by the power of the Holy Spirit. The resurrection is not simply a reversal of death. It is the introduction of a new, indestructible life. The Spirit is the agent by whom this new life bursts forth from the tomb.

The bodily resurrection of Jesus is supported by multiple lines of evidence: the empty tomb discovered by women, the repeated appearances to individuals and groups, the transformation of the disciples from fearful to bold witnesses, and the preaching of the resurrection in the very city where Jesus had been executed and buried. The Holy Spirit, who raised Him, also bears witness to the resurrection through these historical realities and through the inspired Scriptures that interpret them.

The resurrection leads to exaltation. Daniel 7:13–14, which we saw earlier, pictures "one like a son of man" being presented before the Ancient of Days and receiving an everlasting kingdom. The New Testament links this to Jesus' ascension.

Acts 1:1–2 says,

In the first book, O Theophilus, I have dealt with all that Jesus began to do and teach, until the day when he was taken up, after he had given commands through the Holy Spirit to the apostles whom he had chosen.

Even in the time between His resurrection and ascension, Jesus gives commands "through the Holy Spirit." The Spirit is still the channel through which the risen Christ instructs His chosen apostles. The Great Commission is not given in isolation from the Spirit but in close connection with His ongoing work.

On the day of Pentecost, Peter explains what has happened:

Being therefore exalted at the right hand of God, and having received from the Father the promise of the Holy Spirit, he has poured out this that you yourselves are seeing and hearing. (Acts 2:33)

Jesus is "exalted at the right hand of God." There He receives from the Father "the promise of the Holy Spirit" and then pours out the Spirit on the first-century believers. The visible and audible manifestations at Pentecost are not uncontrolled experiences. They are the Spirit's testimony that Jesus has been enthroned as Lord and Messiah.

Peter's conclusion is unmistakable:

Let all the house of Israel therefore know for certain that God has made him both Lord and Christ, this Jesus whom you crucified. (Acts 2:36)

The outpouring of the Spirit is the public announcement, by divine action, that Jesus has been installed as Lord and Christ. The same Spirit who foretold His coming, who brought about His conception, who anointed His ministry, who strengthened Him in obedience, and who raised Him from the dead now testifies to His exaltation.

This means that the Holy Spirit's primary role in this age is not to draw attention to Himself but to bear witness to the glory of the risen and exalted Christ. When we read Acts and the epistles, we see that the Spirit empowers the apostles to preach Jesus, to explain His death and resurrection, to call people to repentance and faith, and to form congregations of believers who confess that Jesus is Lord.

The Holy Spirit and the Glory of Jesus for Believers Today

Although this chapter focuses on Jesus rather than on Christians directly, we cannot ignore the practical implications. The Holy Spirit's relationship to Jesus is the foundation for His relationship to us. The same Spirit who spoke through the prophets, overshadowed Mary, descended on Jesus, empowered His ministry, and raised Him from the dead now speaks to us through the completed Scriptures and calls us to acknowledge Jesus as Lord and Christ.

The Spirit does not give new revelations about Christ that contradict or go beyond what He has already given in the inspired Word. Instead, He uses that Word to open our eyes to the glory of the Son. He confronts us with the evidence that Jesus fulfills the prophecies, that He truly died for our sins, that He really rose from the dead, and that He is now exalted at the right hand of Jehovah.

When a person truly repents and trusts in Christ, this is not a mere human decision produced by clever arguments or emotional pressure. It is the result of the Holy Spirit using the Word to bring conviction of sin, to reveal the beauty and sufficiency of Christ, and to draw the heart to Jehovah. The Spirit's witness is centered on Jesus. He does not magnify the human messenger. He magnifies the Son of God.

For believers, understanding the Spirit's role in the life of Jesus guards us against serious errors. Some groups virtually ignore the Holy Spirit, as if He were an optional doctrine. Others try to separate the Spirit from Christ, chasing experiences and phenomena that are disconnected from the clear teaching of Scripture. Still others focus on Jesus but in a way that minimizes or distorts the Spirit's testimony.

Scripture gives us a balanced and powerful picture. The Holy Spirit is the divine Person who has always been at work to reveal, authenticate, and glorify Jesus Christ. To honor the Spirit rightly is to receive His witness to the Son in the Scriptures. To honor the Son rightly is to recognize that everything He did, from incarnation to exaltation, was in perfect unity with and often explicitly "through" the Holy Spirit.

As we move through the rest of this book, we will see more details about the Holy Spirit's work in the apostles, the early church, and believers today. But everything begins here, with the Holy Spirit and Jesus Christ. The Spirit announces Him, brings Him into the world, anoints Him, empowers Him, supports His perfect obedience, participates in His sacrificial offering, raises Him, and then publicly confirms His exaltation.

This is why Christians can have unshakable confidence in Jesus. Our faith does not rest on human tradition or religious emotion. It rests on the unified work of Jehovah, His Son, and the Holy Spirit. The Spirit Himself has woven the history of Jesus Christ into the very fabric of Scripture and into the very center of the Father's plan. To listen to the Spirit is to listen to the testimony that Jesus is Lord and Christ, the only Savior, and the One to whom all authority in heaven and on earth has been given.

CHAPTER 5 The Holy Spirit and the Apostles

The apostles occupy a role in Christian history that no one else can ever share. They are personally chosen by Jesus Christ, eyewitnesses of His resurrection, and specially equipped by the Holy Spirit to lay the foundation of the Christian congregation and to deliver the final, complete revelation of God's will in the New Testament Scriptures. If we confuse their unique, once-for-history experience of the Holy Spirit with what believers experience today, we will end up with serious doctrinal errors, including the false idea of a literal indwelling of the Holy Spirit in every Christian and the mistaken expectation that apostolic signs and wonders should continue as normal features of church life.

Edward D. Andrews

The Holy Spirit's work in the apostles was powerful, supernatural, and unmistakable. He came upon them, filled them, guided them, and spoke through them so that they could bear authoritative witness to Christ and write the inspired books of the New Testament. At the same time, this work was strictly tied to the foundational period of the church. When the last apostle died and the New Testament writings were complete, the Spirit's direct revelatory and miraculous ministry of that kind ended. He now continues His work fully and sufficiently through the Spirit-inspired Word that those same apostles and their close associates wrote.

In this chapter we will trace the Spirit's relationship to the apostles from Jesus' promises in the Upper Room, through Pentecost and the spread of the gospel, to the completion of the New Testament and the close of the apostolic age. Along the way, we will pay special attention to Romans 8:11 and other texts that are frequently misused to support the idea of a literal indwelling of the Holy Spirit, showing instead that they fit perfectly with the truth that the Spirit guides, assures, and strengthens us today through His completed Word, not by moving into our bodies as an inner Person.

The Promise of the Spirit to the Apostles

On the night before His execution, Jesus spoke directly and intimately to the eleven faithful apostles. In John 14–16 He prepares them for His departure and promises them "another Helper," the Holy Spirit. These promises are often lifted out of their setting and applied as if they were general statements about all believers in every age, but they must first be read in their concrete, historical context.

Jesus says,

If you love me, you will keep my commandments. And I will ask the Father, and he will give you another Helper, that he may be with you forever; the Spirit of truth, whom the world cannot receive, because it does not see him or know him. But you know him because he dwells with you and will be in you.

The "you" in this passage is first and foremost the apostolic group sitting in that Upper Room. They are the ones Jesus has personally chosen, trained, and prepared to be His witnesses. When He says that the Spirit "dwells with you and will be in you," He is describing the special relationship the Helper will have with this core group as He equips them to remember, understand, and proclaim everything Christ has taught.

We must not read this as a technical statement about the Holy Spirit literally entering each believer as an inner guest. The language "with you" and "in you" is covenantal and representative, not spatial. It means that the apostles and, by extension, the true Christian congregation are the sphere where the Spirit will be at work; they will be the community through whom He speaks and in whom His revealed truth is lodged. The world cannot receive Him because it rejects Christ and His Word. The apostles "know" Him because they have walked with Jesus, seen His works done by the Spirit, and will soon experience the Spirit's powerful arrival at Pentecost.

In John 14:26 Jesus adds,

But the Helper, the Holy Spirit, whom the Father will send in my name, that one will teach you all things and bring to your remembrance all that I have said to you.

Again, the "you" here are the apostles. The promise that the Spirit will "teach you all things" and "bring to your remembrance all that I have said to you" is not a general promise that every Christian will receive secret personal instruction or guaranteed perfect memory.

It is a promise that the apostles will be enabled to recall and accurately transmit Jesus' teaching. This directly undergirds the reliability of the Gospels and the apostolic writings.

In John 16:13 Jesus continues,

When he, the Spirit of truth, comes, he will guide you into all the truth, for he will not speak from himself, but whatever he hears he will speak, and he will declare to you the things that are coming.

Once more, this is first and primarily an apostolic promise. The Spirit will guide them "into all the truth" by revealing and explaining the fullness of Christ's work, not by giving each future believer a private stream of revelations. He will "declare to you the things that are coming," which we later see in inspired prophetic writings such as those of Paul, Peter, and John.

These passages show that Jesus promised the Holy Spirit to the apostles in a unique, foundational way. The Spirit's relationship to them is not a model for some mystical indwelling in every believer but a guarantee that the apostolic witness would be accurate, complete, and fully guided by God.

The Day of Pentecost and the Apostolic Foundation

After His resurrection, Jesus told the apostles not to depart from Jerusalem but to wait for "the promise of the Father." He said they would be "baptized with the Holy Spirit not many days from now" and that they would receive power when the Holy Spirit came upon them so that they could be His witnesses in Jerusalem, Judea, Samaria, and to the remotest part of the earth.

Acts 2 shows the fulfillment. On the day of Pentecost, they are all together when a sound like a violent rushing wind fills the house.

Tongues as of fire appear and rest on each one of them, and they are all filled with the Holy Spirit and begin to speak in other languages as the Spirit gives them utterance.

Several key truths are anchored here.

First, this is a historical, public, once-for-history event, not a private experience repeated in every believer. The sound, the visible tongues as of fire, and the sudden ability to speak in real foreign languages are all signs that Jehovah has launched a new stage in His purpose. This is the fulfillment of Joel's promise that He would pour out His Spirit, and of John the Baptist's announcement that the Coming One would baptize with the Holy Spirit.

Second, the focus is on the apostles' role as witnesses. The Spirit gives them languages so they can declare "the mighty works of God" to Jews from every nation gathered in Jerusalem. Peter stands up, explains what is happening, preaches Jesus' death, resurrection, and exaltation, and calls the crowd to repentance and baptism. The miracle of tongues serves the proclamation of the gospel, not private devotion.

Third, being "filled with the Holy Spirit" here does not mean that the Spirit has taken up permanent residence inside their bodies. It refers to being taken under His direct control and empowered for a specific task at that moment. This is shown by the fact that the same apostles are "filled with the Holy Spirit" again in Acts 4:31 when they pray and then speak the Word of God with boldness. If "filling" meant a once-for-all indwelling, they could not be "filled" repeatedly. Instead, Scripture uses "filling" as language for special, intense empowerment for particular occasions.

Pentecost, then, is the Spirit's powerful public endorsement of the apostolic band and the beginning of their worldwide mission. It is not the pattern for continuing personal "Spirit baptisms" in every generation.

The Spirit's Power in Apostolic Preaching and Miracles

From Pentecost onward, the book of Acts shows the Holy Spirit as the One who energizes the apostles' preaching and confirms their message with signs and wonders. The emphasis is always on the Word and on the historical reality of Christ's resurrection, with the miracles serving as divine credentials.

In Acts 2, Peter's Spirit-empowered sermon cuts his hearers to the heart. He proclaims that God has made Jesus, whom they crucified, both Lord and Christ. About three thousand respond, repent, and are baptized. It is the Spirit's work through the preached Word that brings conviction. The miracle of languages simply draws attention and testifies that Jehovah Himself is behind this message.

In Acts 3, a man lame from birth is healed at the temple gate. Peter explains that this miracle is done in the name of Jesus Christ the Nazarene and uses it to preach again about repentance and the forgiveness of sins. Acts 4 describes the authorities commanding the apostles to be silent. After being threatened, they gather with other believers, pray, and the place is shaken. They are all filled with the Holy Spirit and speak the Word of God with boldness. Once more, filling equals powerful boldness in proclaiming the gospel, not some private sense of the Spirit dwelling inside.

Acts 5:12 states that many signs and wonders were done at the hands of the apostles and that people brought the sick out so that even Peter's shadow might fall on some of them. These miracles are extraordinary and clearly apostolic in character. They demonstrate that the risen Christ is working through His chosen witnesses and authenticate their teaching as divine truth.

None of this suggests that every believer in every era will or should perform miracles. The pattern in Acts is that the apostles and certain closely connected individuals are granted miraculous powers during the foundational stage of the church, while the majority of believers serve in other, non-miraculous ways. Later New Testament letters show that miraculous gifts themselves are temporary and tied to the period when revelation is still being given.

The key point is that the Holy Spirit's power in the apostles is always directed toward one thing: testifying to Jesus Christ and establishing the authority of the Word. He is not given to produce spectacles for their own sake, nor to give believers a permanent, internal feeling, but to drive and confirm the apostolic proclamation of the gospel.

The Spirit's Guidance of Apostolic Mission and Decisions

The apostles did not design the mission of the church by human strategy. The Holy Spirit personally directed where they should go, when they should move, and how major doctrinal issues should be decided. This direct guidance again shows the unique relationship between the Spirit and the apostles.

In Acts 13, while prophets and teachers in Antioch are ministering to Jehovah and fasting, the Holy Spirit says,

Set apart for me Barnabas and Saul for the work to which I have called them.

After further fasting and prayer, they lay hands on Barnabas and Saul, and the two men are sent out "by the Holy Spirit." This is not a vague sense of "leading." It is a specific command with clear content: which men, what work, and when to send them. The Spirit speaks in a way that leaves no doubt.

In Acts 16, Paul and his companions are "forbidden by the Holy Spirit to speak the word in Asia" and when they try to go into Bithynia, "the Spirit of Jesus did not allow them." The result is that they reach Troas, where Paul receives the vision of the Macedonian man calling them to come over and help. Again, the Spirit is not merely influencing feelings. He is giving precise, directional guidance about where the gospel should be preached at that stage.

The clearest example of the Spirit's role in decision making appears in Acts 15, at the Jerusalem gathering where the apostles and elders consider whether Gentile believers must be circumcised and keep the law of Moses. After hearing testimonies and considering the evidence, James proposes a decision that respects the gospel of grace and preserves unity. The letter sent to the Gentile congregations begins with the words,

For it seemed good to the Holy Spirit and to us to lay on you no greater burden than these essentials.

This is not pious language thrown in after a human compromise. It reflects the reality that the apostles are consciously aware of the Spirit's guidance in their deliberations. They know that their final judgment aligns with what He has shown and confirmed.

This does not mean that every church board or committee today can claim, "it seemed good to the Holy Spirit and to us," as though human impressions or consensus were equal to apostolic guidance. The apostles were inspired, foundational witnesses. Their Spirit-guided decisions are now preserved for us in Scripture. Today, the Spirit leads congregations not by fresh, extra-biblical revelations but by the sound application of the written Word He has already given.

The Spirit and Apostolic Revelation and Scripture

The central way the Holy Spirit works through the apostles is by giving them revelation and then preserving that revelation in written form as the New Testament. Jesus' promises in the Upper Room about teaching, reminding, and guiding into all the truth find their concrete fulfillment in the apostolic preaching and the inspired books they produced.

Peter explains this in a general way when he says,

No prophecy of Scripture comes from someone's own interpretation. For no prophecy was ever brought by the will of man, but men spoke from God as they were moved by the Holy Spirit.

This principle applies not only to Old Testament prophets but also to apostolic writing. The Holy Spirit moves the human authors so that what they write is truly their own style and vocabulary, yet at the same time it is fully the Word of God, free from error in everything it affirms.

Paul describes something similar in 1 Corinthians 2. He explains that God has revealed the things He has prepared for those who love Him, not through human wisdom but "through the Spirit." The Spirit searches the deep things of God and reveals them to the apostles. Paul says,

We received not the spirit of the world, but the Spirit which is from God, that we might know the things that have been freely given to us by God; which things also we speak, not in words taught by human wisdom, but in words taught by the Spirit.

Here the "we" is apostolic. The Spirit has given them not only the content but also the words in which that content is to be expressed. This does not mean mechanical dictation, but it does mean that the final product is exactly what the Spirit intends.

When believers today correctly understand Scripture, they are not receiving new revelations. They are grasping, through normal human study and reverent attention, what the Spirit already revealed once for all to the apostles and their close associates. The Spirit's revelatory work is finished; His interpretive role is exercised through the inspired text and careful, grammatical-historical exegesis.

This is why we must reject the idea that Christians need an inner mystical "illumination" beyond the Word. The Spirit's "illumination" is not some extra meaning whispered into the heart. It is the clarity and force with which the written Word comes to bear on the mind and conscience as we work to understand it according to sound principles of interpretation.

The Spirit's Gifts Through the Apostles

One of the most misunderstood aspects of the Holy Spirit's work in the apostolic age is the distribution of miraculous gifts. Many today assume that every believer in every era should expect spectacular manifestations as a normal part of life. The New Testament shows something very different.

In Acts 8, when the Samaritans believe the gospel preached by Philip and are baptized, the apostles in Jerusalem hear the news and send Peter and John. These apostles pray for the Samaritans to receive the Holy Spirit, "for he had not yet fallen upon any of them; they had simply been baptized in the name of the Lord Jesus." Then they lay their hands on them, and the Samaritans receive the Holy Spirit in a visible way. Simon the sorcerer sees that the Spirit is given through the laying on of the apostles' hands and tries to buy this authority, which Peter strongly rebukes.

The key observation here is that the Samaritan believers did not receive these visible, miraculous operations of the Spirit at the moment of baptism. They received them when apostles came, prayed, and laid hands on them. The phrase "receive the Holy Spirit" in this context refers to receiving extraordinary gifts, not to a general, invisible relationship with God.

A similar pattern occurs in Acts 19. Paul meets some disciples in Ephesus who have only known John's baptism. After explaining Christ to them, he baptizes them in the name of the Lord Jesus. Then, when Paul lays his hands on them, the Holy Spirit comes upon them, and they speak in tongues and prophesy. Again, the visible gifts are conferred through the hands of an apostle.

Paul reminds Timothy to "kindle afresh the gift of God which is in you through the laying on of my hands." This shows that even the spiritual gift Timothy had came by apostolic mediation.

From these passages we can safely conclude several things. Miraculous gifts were not universally given to all believers. They were distributed at the Spirit's will, often through the hands of apostles. They served to confirm new revelation and to build up the early congregations before the New Testament Scriptures were complete. Once the last apostle died and no further laying on of apostolic hands was possible, the supply line for these sign gifts ceased.

This has nothing to do with the Holy Spirit withdrawing from the church. It simply means that His mode of operation has changed in line with the completion of the canon. He no longer confirms new revelations with signs because no new revelation is being given. Instead, He applies the once-for-all revelation already recorded in Scripture.

Edward D. Andrews

Romans 8:11 and the Apostolic Witness to Resurrection

Romans chapter 8 is a favorite chapter for those who argue that the Holy Spirit literally dwells inside the bodies of believers. Verse 11 is especially used as a proof-text:

If the Spirit of him who raised Jesus from the dead dwells in you, he who raised Christ Jesus from the dead will also give life to your mortal bodies through his Spirit who dwells in you.

At first glance, phrases like "dwells in you" sound like strong support for the indwelling idea. But when we apply careful, grammatical-historical interpretation, we see that Paul is not describing a mystical, personal residence of the Spirit inside believers. Instead, he is describing their new standing and hope in relation to the Spirit's resurrection power.

The first part of the verse identifies the Spirit as "the Spirit of him who raised Jesus from the dead." This is the same Spirit whose work the apostles boldly preached in Acts. Peter declares that God raised Jesus and that the Spirit is given as witness to this fact. The apostles are the Spirit-empowered witnesses that Christ is alive and exalted.

When Paul says that this Spirit "dwells in you," he is not giving a spatial analysis of where the Spirit is located. He is using relational language to say that believers now belong to the realm, or sphere, where the Spirit's resurrection power is operative. They are "in Christ" and therefore "in the Spirit" rather than "in the flesh." The Spirit is said to "dwell" in them because they have embraced the gospel the Spirit gave, have aligned themselves with the risen Christ, and stand under the influence and authority of the Spirit's revealed truth.

88

The second part of the verse looks to the future: God "will also give life to your mortal bodies through his Spirit who dwells in you." This is a promise of bodily resurrection, not of ongoing internal renovation during this life through some inner indwelling presence. The guarantee that our mortal bodies will one day be raised and transformed rests on the fact that the Spirit has already raised Jesus and that we now belong to Him by faith.

In other words, Romans 8:11 is about **assurance of future bodily resurrection in union with Christ**, grounded in the Spirit's past work in raising Jesus and His present authority over believers through the gospel. It is not a technical statement about the Spirit moving inside human bodies as if He were a resident occupant.

Apostolically, this matches perfectly with how the Spirit's work is proclaimed in Acts. The apostles testify that God raised Jesus through the Spirit and that this resurrection guarantees a future resurrection for all who belong to Him. The Spirit's "dwelling" language must be read against this backdrop of covenant relationship and resurrection hope, not imported into a theology of literal indwelling.

The End of the Apostolic Age and the Ongoing Work of the Spirit

By the end of the first century, the apostles had completed the task the Holy Spirit gave them. The gospel had been carried from Jerusalem to Judea, Samaria, and far into the Gentile world. Congregations had been established, elderships appointed, and the major doctrinal issues facing Jew and Gentile believers clarified under the Spirit's guidance. Most importantly, the full body of authoritative teaching needed for the church's life had been delivered and committed to writing.

The last surviving apostle, John, wrote his Gospel, letters, and Revelation near the end of the century. With his death, the unique apostolic office passed from the scene. No one today is an apostle in this sense. No one has seen the risen Christ with physical eyes, heard His voice in person, or been directly commissioned by Him in the way the Twelve and Paul were.

With the close of the apostolic age, the particular ways the Holy Spirit had been working in and through the apostles also ceased. There are no longer new revelations, no longer inspired decisions like Acts 15, no longer an ongoing stream of Spirit-given Scripture. The miraculous sign gifts that accompanied and confirmed that revelatory period faded as their purpose was fulfilled.

However, the Holy Spirit Himself has not ceased working. He continues His ministry through the complete, sufficient, inerrant Scriptures that He inspired. Paul writes that all Scripture is breathed out by God and is profitable for teaching, reproof, correction, and training in righteousness so that the man of God may be complete, equipped for every good work. If Scripture, breathed out by the Spirit, can fully equip the believer for every good work, then nothing more is needed.

Today the Spirit does not indwell believers as an internal Person, whispering new meanings or secret directions. Instead, He speaks through the written Word. When believers read, hear, and obey Scripture, they are responding to the Spirit. When congregations measure their teaching and practice by the apostolic writings, they are being guided by the Spirit. When the gospel is preached from the Bible and sinners are convicted and brought to repentance and faith, that is the Holy Spirit using His own Word to bring life.

To "walk according to the Spirit" in our day means to order our lives by the teaching the Spirit has given in Scripture. To "set the mind on the things of the Spirit" means to fill our thoughts with those truths and values revealed in the Bible. There is no need to search for inward visions, voices, or impressions. The Spirit's voice is already perfectly clear in the pages of the Old and New Testaments.

Understanding the Holy Spirit's work with the apostles, therefore, does two things for us. It strengthens our confidence in the New Testament as the fully trustworthy Word of God, delivered by men whom the Spirit guided in a unique way. And it protects us from being misled by modern claims to new revelations, continuing apostolic authority, or mystical indwelling experiences that have no basis in the completed revelation of God.

The same Holy Spirit who came upon the apostles at Pentecost, who empowered their preaching and miracles, who guided their decisions, who gave them words to write, and who guaranteed the resurrection of Jesus now works through their completed writings to build, correct, and comfort the people of God until Christ returns and raises all who belong to Him.

CHAPTER 6 The Holy Spirit and the Apostolic Church

The relationship between the Holy Spirit and the apostolic church was utterly unique. It cannot be reproduced, revived, or extended into later centuries without seriously distorting Scripture. The first congregations lived in a time when Jesus had only recently ascended, the apostles were still alive, much of the New Testament had not yet been written, and the message about Christ was still being announced for the very first time in city after city. In that transitional setting the Holy Spirit acted in ways that were temporary and foundational: He empowered apostles and selected coworkers with miraculous gifts, He confirmed new revelation with signs and wonders, He directed missionary journeys with specific commands, and He enabled inspired decisions and writings that would become our permanent standard.

Today, the Holy Spirit does not work in the same way. He does not give new revelations. He does not scatter miraculous gifts across congregations as a normal feature of Christian life. He does not personally indwell believers as an inner, mystical Presence. Instead, He now works through the complete, inerrant Scriptures that He Himself inspired. The difference between the apostolic age and our own is not that the Spirit has lost power, but that His plan has moved from **foundation-laying** to **building on the finished foundation.**

To see this clearly we must trace how the Spirit related to the apostolic church and how the completion of the New Testament changed the way He works among God's people.

The Unique Role of the Holy Spirit in the Apostolic Church

The apostolic church lived in a time of **partial revelation.** The death, resurrection, and exaltation of Jesus had taken place, but the full explanation of these events had not yet been written down. Congregations could not open a bound New Testament and turn to Romans or Ephesians. Many of the letters we now take for granted had not yet been authored. Some congregations had one or two inspired letters; others had none at first.

Because of this, the Holy Spirit sustained a special relationship with the apostolic church that He does not sustain with the church today. Paul describes this transitional situation in 1 Corinthians 13:

For we know in part and we prophesy in part, but when the perfect comes, the partial will pass away.

Here Paul contrasts two conditions. On the one hand is **knowing and prophesying "in part"**—a situation where revelation is still being given piece by piece, and where miraculous gifts play a major role. On the other hand is the arrival of "the perfect," at which point "the partial will pass away."

This is not a contrast between earthly life and heavenly glory, as if Paul meant, "Now we have spiritual gifts, but in heaven we will not need them." The entire letter of 1 Corinthians deals with life in the congregation now, not describing life in heaven. The "partial" refers to the fragmentary and provisional character of revelation during the apostolic period. The "perfect" refers to the completed, fully sufficient revelation of the gospel and Christian life—the mature state of the faith once the New Testament writings were finished and circulated.

When that complete body of teaching—the "perfect law of liberty," the perfect gospel, the finished New Testament—had been given, the partial forms of revelation and confirmation, such as prophecy, tongues, and knowledge-gifts, passed away because their purpose had been fulfilled. Jealousy and confusion over gifts in Corinth show why such temporary provisions could not be the lasting pattern for the church.

The apostolic church therefore experienced the Holy Spirit in a way that combined two things: first, the same basic realities that every age must have—a true gospel, repentance, faith, and obedience; and second, a layer of temporary, miraculous provisions required because the New Testament was not yet complete.

Spiritual Gifts as Foundational, Not Permanent

The clearest picture of these temporary provisions appears in 1 Corinthians 12. Paul writes that "to each is given the manifestation of the Spirit for the common good," and then lists gifts such as wisdom, knowledge, faith, healings, miracles, prophecy, discerning of spirits, various kinds of tongues, and the interpretation of tongues. He concludes that "all these are empowered by one and the same Spirit, who apportions to each one individually as he wills."

Several truths emerge when we read this carefully in its first-century setting.

First, these gifts are **manifestations** of the Spirit, not the Spirit Himself. They are outward activities and abilities by which the Spirit makes His presence known in a particular congregation. They are not permanent inner possessions that every believer carries for life.

Second, the gifts are distributed according to the Spirit's will, not according to personal desire or supposed levels of spirituality. Some believers in Corinth coveted the showier gifts, especially tongues, but Paul reminds them that not all are apostles, not all are prophets, not all speak with tongues. The distribution itself is part of the Spirit's design for that time.

Third, the gifts are specifically aimed at **building up the body of Christ** while revelation is still in progress. Ephesians 4 explains that Christ gave apostles, prophets, evangelists, shepherds, and teachers "for the equipping of the holy ones, for the work of ministry, for the building up of the body of Christ, until we all attain to the unity of the faith and of the knowledge of the Son of God, to a mature man." In the earliest period, prophetic messages, Spirit-given words of knowledge, and tongues with interpretation all served as temporary scaffolding while the permanent structure—the apostolic doctrine— was being delivered and stabilized.

Fourth, the gifts are repeatedly tied to the **foundational stage** of the church. Paul says the household of God is built on the foundation of the apostles and prophets, Christ Jesus Himself being the cornerstone. A foundation is laid once. You do not relaid it in every generation. Likewise, you do not need continuous new prophets, new tongues, and new miraculous signs once the foundation of doctrine and witness is complete.

This is why the Spirit's gifts are never presented as a permanent, unending feature of normal church life. There are no instructions in the later New Testament letters telling believers in future generations to seek tongues or prophecy. Instead, the emphasis steadily shifts to guarding the deposit of teaching already given, to the reading and explanation of Scripture, and to the appointment of qualified elders and deacons who apply that teaching.

In other words, the gifts were real, powerful, and absolutely necessary for the first-century church; but they were also **temporary tools**, not abiding structures.

The Baptism in the Holy Spirit and the Birth of the Church

The central public event that introduces this age of miraculous provision is the baptism in the Holy Spirit at Pentecost. Acts 2 records that when the day of Pentecost had fully come, the disciples were together in one place. A sound like a violent rushing wind filled the house, tongues as of fire appeared and rested on each one, and they were all filled with the Holy Spirit and began to speak in other languages as the Spirit gave them utterance.

This is not a private inward sensation. It is a public, audible, and visible event. Jews from many nations hear the apostles speaking in their own native languages, declaring the mighty works of God. Peter stands up and explains that this is the fulfillment of the promise that God would pour out His Spirit. He connects it to the resurrection and exaltation of Jesus: the risen Christ has received from the Father the promise of the Holy Spirit and has poured out what the crowd is seeing and hearing.

Several aspects of this event must be underlined.

Pentecost is **unrepeatable.** Jesus had told the apostles that they would be baptized with the Holy Spirit "not many days from now." Peter later recalls this promise when the Spirit falls on the household of Cornelius and says that the Gentile experience is "just as on us at the beginning." The wording "at the beginning" shows that Pentecost is the starting point, not a pattern to be reproduced indefinitely.

The purpose of this baptism is **empowerment for witness** and **validation of the apostolic message**, not a mystical inner cleansing or a second blessing for private devotion. Jesus had already described the apostles as "clean" because of the word He had spoken to them. The baptism in the Holy Spirit equips them to proclaim that word with boldness and to authenticate it before Jews and Gentiles with miraculous signs.

The event does **not** teach that every believer in every age will be "baptized with the Holy Spirit" in the Pentecost sense. The New Testament never commands believers to seek Spirit baptism, never presents it as a normal individual experience, and never links it to modern charismatic phenomena. Instead, it treats Pentecost and the similar outpouring at Cornelius' house as epoch-making acts of Christ to launch the church and to show that Jews and Gentiles stand on equal footing in the one body.

When we limit the baptism in the Holy Spirit to its proper historical place, we protect ourselves from the error of chasing experiences that Scripture never promises and from confusing the foundation of the church with the normal life of the church.

The Spirit's Work Through the Apostles in the Congregations

The Holy Spirit did not relate to the apostolic church in a vague, general way. He acted through identifiable men, primarily the apostles, in specific ways that can be traced in the book of Acts.

He confirmed the apostolic preaching with miracles. Acts 5:12 tells us that "at the hands of the apostles many signs and wonders were taking place among the people." The healing of the lame man at the temple gate, the casting out of demons, the raising of the dead—all these acts are not random miracles but deliberate signs that Jehovah is behind the apostolic message about Christ. The miracles never stand by themselves; they serve the Word.

He directed the outreach of the church. In Acts 13, as certain men in Antioch are ministering to Jehovah and fasting, the Holy Spirit says, "Set apart for me Barnabas and Saul for the work to which I have called them." The congregation obeys, and Barnabas and Saul are sent out "by the Holy Spirit." Later, in Acts 16, the Spirit forbids Paul and his companions to speak the word in Asia and does not permit them to enter Bithynia. This specific guidance results in the gospel crossing into Macedonia.

He participated directly in crucial doctrinal decisions. At the Jerusalem gathering in Acts 15, where the question of circumcision for Gentile believers is addressed, the apostles and elders weigh the evidence, listen to Peter and Paul, and search the Scriptures. Their final letter to the Gentile congregations begins, "For it seemed good to the Holy Spirit and to us to lay upon you no greater burden than these essentials." They know that the Spirit has guided them to a decision that reflects His will, and that decision is preserved in Scripture as binding for the church of all ages.

He used the apostles as channels for **miraculous gifts** in others. In Samaria, believers had accepted the word of God and been baptized in the name of the Lord Jesus, yet the Holy Spirit had not yet fallen upon any of them in a visible, miraculous way. When Peter and John come from Jerusalem, they pray and lay hands on them, and then the Samaritans receive the Holy Spirit. Simon the sorcerer sees that the Spirit is bestowed through the laying on of the apostles' hands and covets this ability.

The same pattern appears at Ephesus when Paul lays his hands on certain disciples, after which the Holy Spirit comes upon them and they speak in tongues and prophesy. Even Timothy is reminded by Paul of "the gift of God" in him through the laying on of the apostle's hands.

This chain of evidence shows that the supernatural distribution of Spirit-given gifts in the apostolic church is tied directly to the apostles' presence and authority. When the last apostle dies, that channel closes. The ordinary life of the church moves forward with the spiritual resources already provided in the completed Scriptures, godly elders, and the normal operations of faith, hope, and love.

The Completion of Revelation and the Passing of the Partial

As the years of the first century passed, the Holy Spirit led the apostles and their close coworkers to commit the essential truths of the gospel, the instructions for congregational life, and the warnings about future dangers to writing. The Gospels, Acts, the letters, and Revelation were not written in one moment. They arose as the Spirit guided real men to address real needs in real congregations. But behind all the variety stands one Author, the Holy Spirit, who ensured that what was written is exactly what Jehovah wanted preserved.

By the time the apostle John wrote his last book near the end of the century, the faith had reached a state of doctrinal completeness. Jude could urge believers to contend earnestly for "the faith which was once for all delivered to the holy ones." The phrase "once for all" indicates a completed act, not an ongoing process.

At that point, what Paul had described as "partial" in 1 Corinthians 13 had given way to "the perfect." The church no longer depended on scattered prophetic utterances to know the will of God. It had in its hands the written, fixed, Spirit-breathed revelation that fully equips the man of God for every good work.

When the perfect, complete revelation is present, the partial, fragmentary forms that helped prepare for it naturally pass away. This is precisely what we see after the apostolic age. Reports of miracles and prophecy become sporadic and confused, often mixed with legend and error. Meanwhile, faithful believers concentrate on copying, studying, and teaching the apostolic writings. The line of real authority runs not through later visions and signs but through the written Word.

It is therefore a serious mistake when modern groups attempt to reproduce the spiritual climate of Corinth or Acts 2 as if that were the permanent pattern. Doing so ignores the Spirit's own movement of history. He Himself replaced the partial with the perfect, the temporary scaffolding with the complete building. To insist on going back to the partial is not spiritual progress but spiritual regression.

Romans 8:11 and the Apostolic Church's Hope

Romans 8 stands at the heart of the New Testament teaching about life "according to the Spirit." Verse 11 is often used to support the idea that the Holy Spirit dwells literally inside believers as an inner Person:

If the Spirit of him who raised Jesus from the dead dwells in you, he who raised Christ Jesus from the dead will also give life to your mortal bodies through his Spirit who dwells in you.

A glance at the language might seem to favor indwelling, but when we place the verse within Paul's argument and within the larger apostolic context, the picture changes.

The "Spirit of him who raised Jesus from the dead" is the same Spirit whose work is proclaimed throughout Acts: He raised Jesus, vindicated Him as Messiah, and empowered the apostles to preach that resurrection. The resurrection of Jesus is a historical event, testified to by witnesses whose minds and lips the Spirit directed.

When Paul says that this Spirit "dwells in you," he is not describing a mystical internal guest. He is describing the believer's **relationship** to that resurrection power and **alignment** with the Spirit's revealed truth. In Romans 8, to be "in the Spirit" is to belong to Christ, to set the mind on the things the Spirit has revealed, and to walk according to that teaching rather than according to the flesh. The "dwelling" language is covenantal and representational: believers are now the people among whom the Spirit's resurrection life and truth are operative.

The promise that God "will also give life to your mortal bodies" points forward to the future resurrection. The Spirit who raised Jesus guarantees that the same kind of bodily resurrection awaits those who belong to Him. This is not a present, ongoing internal process of mystical transformation; it is a future, decisive act when Christ returns.

The apostolic church clung to this hope. They did not rest their confidence on feelings of inner Presence but on the solid historical fact that Christ had been raised and on the Spirit-given promise that they too would be raised. Romans 8:11, rightly understood, strengthens that hope. It does **not** teach that the Holy Spirit literally inhabits the physical bodies of believers today.

Excursion: "Holy Spirit" and Luke 11:13

The expression "holy spirit" in the Greek New Testament appears many times, sometimes with the definite article ("the Holy Spirit") and sometimes without it. Because English uses the article differently than Greek, readers can be misled into thinking that when the Greek lacks "the," the phrase must refer to something more general, such as a holy attitude or a holy influence, rather than to the Holy Spirit Himself.

Greek, however, can express definiteness in other ways. Nouns used with certain prepositions, or nouns that are well known in the context, can be definite even without the article. Students of Greek grammar have long recognized that "holy spirit" can function as a definite expression in contexts where the subject is clearly the third Person of the Godhead.

Luke 11:13 reads,

If you then, being evil, know how to give good gifts to your children, how much more will your heavenly Father give the Holy Spirit to those who ask him?

Here the phrase "Holy Spirit" lacks the article in Greek, but the context shows that Jesus is not speaking of a vague "holy quality" or of human spirit. He is speaking of the divine Spirit as a gift from the Father. The parallel in Matthew 7:11 uses the phrase "good things," which helps us see that Luke's wording focuses on the supreme good gift, the Holy Spirit.

What does this promise mean? In the immediate historical setting, Jesus is addressing disciples who will live to see Pentecost and the outpouring of miraculous gifts. For them, asking the Father and receiving the Holy Spirit includes the expectation of those extraordinary manifestations that would mark the beginning of the apostolic age. In that sense the verse points forward to the same reality that appears in John 7:38–39, where Jesus speaks of rivers of living water flowing from the one who believes, and the Gospel writer explains that He said this about the Spirit who was to be received after Jesus was glorified.

At the same time, Luke 11:13 must be read in harmony with everything Scripture later teaches about the Spirit's work after the apostolic period. The promise is not that every believer in every age will receive miraculous powers if only he asks hard enough. Nor is it a guarantee of a mystical inner indwelling. Rather, it assures disciples that the Father is generous in giving His Spirit in the way appropriate to His plan at each stage of history. In the first century that included prophetic gifts, tongues, and miracles; in our age it includes the full benefit of the Spirit's completed revelation in Scripture.

Some appeal to the longer ending of Mark (Mark 16:9–20) to support the idea that signs such as snake handling, drinking poison without harm, and healing the sick should characterize believers in every era. But serious textual and contextual study shows that these verses are not part of Mark's original Gospel and, even if they were, they would describe the signs accompanying the earliest preaching of the gospel, not a permanent pattern for all time. The safest and most reverent course is to let the clear teaching of Acts and the letters govern our expectations: miraculous signs belonged to the foundational age and faded as the apostolic witness became fixed in written form.

So when believers today read Luke 11:13 and ask the Father for the Holy Spirit, they are not asking for new revelations or spectacular gifts. They are asking that He help them receive, understand, and obey the Spirit-inspired Word; that He open doors for that Word to spread; and that He strengthen them to live out the gospel faithfully. The answer to such prayers comes as the same Holy Spirit who once gave tongues and prophecy now uses the Scriptures He inspired to shape minds, convict hearts, and guide obedient steps.

The Holy Spirit and the Church Today

Once we understand how the Spirit related to the apostolic church, the difference in our own situation becomes clear and reassuring. We are not at a disadvantage because we do not see tongues of fire or hear audible commands. On the contrary, we stand in a position of great privilege. We possess the complete New Testament along with the Old, all preserved by God's care.

The Holy Spirit today does not indwell Christians in a literal, personal way. He does not whisper new meanings into our minds or override the need for careful study. He does not test us by sending hardships or orchestrating difficulties to refine us. Trials come from a fallen world, from human imperfection, and from the malice of Satan and demons, not from Jehovah. What the Spirit does is far better: He has given us a fully sufficient, written revelation, and He works through that revelation whenever it is rightly read, explained, believed, and obeyed.

THE HOLY SPIRIT

When congregations gather to read Scripture publicly, the Holy Spirit is at work through that inspired text. When a teacher explains a passage accurately, following sound grammatical-historical principles, the Spirit's meaning is opened up, not because the teacher has a private pipeline, but because the Spirit's words in Scripture are being allowed to speak for themselves. When a believer meditates on the Word and adjusts his life accordingly, the Spirit is guiding him—not by an inward nudge, but by the objective authority of the written Word.

The apostolic church needed visions, prophetic utterances, and miraculous signs because the revelation of Christ was still in the process of being given. We do not need those things because we have what they did not yet have: the completed canon. The Spirit has not retreated; He has **shifted His focus**. Instead of standing behind new speeches and new signs, He now stands behind the Bible, pressing its message on conscience and mind.

The more we grasp this, the less attracted we will be to modern counterfeit claims of new prophecies, new tongues, and new revelations. We will see such claims not as deeper spirituality but as a subtle denial that the Spirit has already spoken clearly and sufficiently in Scripture. True spirituality in this age is not measured by unusual experiences but by humble submission to the Word the Holy Spirit has already given.

The Holy Spirit and the apostolic church, then, belong together in a unique and unrepeatable chapter of God's plan. The same Spirit who empowered the apostles, distributed gifts, and guided the first congregations has now inscribed their testimony in the pages of the New Testament. He calls us, not to seek another Pentecost, but to build our lives and churches on that finished, Spirit-breathed foundation until Christ returns and the resurrection promised in Romans 8:11 becomes reality for all who belong to Him.

CHAPTER 7 The Holy Spirit and the World

When people speak about the Holy Spirit and the world, they often drift into one of two extremes. Some imagine the Spirit as an invisible, irresistible force sweeping through humanity, secretly changing hearts apart from any contact with Scripture. Others reduce His present work almost to nothing, as if He did everything in the first century and now merely watches from a distance. Both views miss the careful balance of the Bible.

Scripture presents the Holy Spirit as actively involved with the world today, yet His activity is precise, ordered, and entirely tied to the revelation He has given. He does not personally indwell unbelievers or believers. He does not whisper new messages or bypass the mind. He does not send hardships or disasters as "tests." Instead,

He works through the Spirit-inspired Word of God, confronting the world with truth, exposing sin, opening the way of salvation, and forming a people who live by that same Word.

To understand this correctly, we must ask a basic question: in what way can one spirit influence another? Once we see the answer, it becomes clear why the Holy Spirit used one kind of influence in the apostolic age and why, in this present age, He works exclusively through the Scriptures.

How One Spirit Influences Another

Human beings are not machines. We are souls—living persons— created to think, to choose, and to respond. When one person influences another, that influence normally comes through ideas, words, and examples. The Bible uses the same pattern when it describes how the Holy Spirit operates.

In principle only two kinds of influence are possible between spirits. One is a direct, overriding control, where the mind and speech of a person are taken over so that what is said and done does not originate in that person's own thinking. Scripture shows that this kind of immediate control did occur in the case of prophets and apostles when they spoke and wrote under inspiration. Jesus told His apostles that when they were brought before rulers, they were not to worry beforehand what they should say,

for it is not you who speak, but the Holy Spirit.

On the day of Pentecost, those present were "filled with the Holy Spirit and began to speak with other tongues, as the Spirit was giving them utterance." Their own minds and mouths were instruments by which the Spirit delivered words and truths that did not come from their natural understanding.

The other kind of influence is rational and moral. It works through information, arguments, warnings, promises, and examples—through words that carry meaning. This is the way teachers influence students, parents influence children, and preachers influence hearers. The mind is not overridden; it is confronted with truth and urged to submit. The Holy Spirit uses this method whenever He works through Scripture.

There is no third way. Either a person is directly controlled, as with inspired prophets and apostles, or he is persuaded and convicted by truth communicated to his mind. The first method was temporary and limited to those whom Jehovah chose as His messengers in the foundational era. The second method is what the Spirit uses now and will continue to use until Christ returns.

The Holy Spirit and the Present Age

In earlier chapters we saw that, in the apostolic age, the Holy Spirit sometimes worked on people immediately, apart from prior study, in order to produce revelation or confirm it with signs and wonders. The apostles were brought under His direct control so that they spoke infallibly in Christ's name and wrote the inspired New Testament Scriptures. That phase of His work was unique and has ceased with the completion of the canon and the death of the last apostle.

The question now is whether the Spirit continues to be a power in this present age and, if so, what kind of power. The answer is that He is deeply active, but **only** through the instrumentality of the Word He inspired. He no longer takes over human minds mechanically; He addresses minds morally and rationally through Scripture.

The world is still divided into two broad groups. There are those who remain unbelieving, "aliens from the commonwealth of Israel," without hope and without God in the world. There are those who have believed and obeyed the gospel and become children of God. The Holy Spirit has a distinct relationship to each group, but in both cases He works by means of the same instrument: the written Word of God.

This chapter will focus primarily on the Spirit's work toward the unbelieving world, then briefly show how the same pattern continues in the lives of believers.

The Spirit's Work of Conviction in the World

Shortly before His arrest, Jesus told the apostles that after His departure He would send the Helper. He said,

And he, when he comes, will convict the world concerning sin and righteousness and judgment; concerning sin, because they do not believe in me; and concerning righteousness, because I go to the Father and you no longer see me; and concerning judgment, because the ruler of this world has been judged.

Many imagine this means that the Spirit moves secretly, from heart to heart, apart from the gospel, producing an inward sensation of guilt or fear. But Jesus explained this promise to men who would soon be preaching and writing under inspiration. The Spirit's "coming" in this context is His arrival at Pentecost, His empowering of the apostolic witness, and His continued work through that same witness as it is now preserved in Scripture.

To "convict" does not mean to generate a vague feeling. It means to present a clear, inescapable case that exposes wrong, vindicates what is right, and announces the outcome. A prosecutor brings conviction by evidence and argument; the Spirit brings conviction by the evidence and argument He has placed in the Word.

He convicts the world **concerning sin** "because they do not believe in" Jesus. The greatest sin is the refusal to believe the gospel. Through the preached and written Word, the Spirit confronts unbelievers with the reality of their rebellion, not only in outward acts but in their rejection of the Son. When Peter preached at Pentecost, he told the crowd that they had crucified the One whom God had made both Lord and Christ. When they were "pierced to the heart," that was the Spirit's conviction working through the message.

He convicts the world **concerning righteousness** "because I go to the Father and you no longer see me." Jesus' resurrection and exaltation show that Jehovah has declared Him righteous and has accepted His sacrifice. The Spirit testifies to this righteousness through apostolic preaching and the New Testament writings. The world's standards of righteousness are exposed as false when they clash with the righteousness revealed in Christ.

He convicts the world **concerning judgment** "because the ruler of this world has been judged." The cross and resurrection are not only about forgiveness; they also mark the defeat of Satan. The Spirit announces this judgment through Scripture, warning that those who persist in following the ruler of this world will share his fate.

Notice that all three aspects of conviction—sin, righteousness, and judgment—are historical and doctrinal truths proclaimed in the gospel. The Spirit does not produce them by mystical impressions. He presses them on the conscience whenever the Bible is opened, explained, and applied.

The Word as the Spirit's Instrument

Because the Spirit now works morally through truth rather than mechanically by control, His primary instrument in the world today is the Bible. All Scripture is "God-breathed." It comes from the Spirit of God and therefore carries His authority. It is profitable for teaching, for reproof, for correction, and for training in righteousness so that the man of God may be complete, fully equipped for every good work.

The Word of God is described as "living and active and sharper than any two-edged sword," piercing to the division of soul and spirit and judging the thoughts and intentions of the heart. That kind of searching power is the Spirit's power, exercised through the words He has breathed out. When people say that the Bible "read" them while they were reading it, they are describing the effect of the Spirit's moral influence operating through written truth.

Because faith comes from hearing, and hearing comes by the Word of Christ, there is no such thing as saving faith produced without the message of Scripture. The Spirit does not plant faith in hearts apart from the Word. He uses the Word to show who God is, what sin is, who Christ is, and what response Jehovah requires.

This is why efforts to separate the Spirit from the Bible are so dangerous. When someone claims to be "led by the Spirit" but sets aside clear biblical teaching, we can be sure that the Spirit is not the one leading. The Spirit never contradicts Himself. The voice we hear in Scripture is His voice, and He has chosen that voice as His only instrument for dealing with the world in this age.

The Spirit's Role in Conversion

Conversion takes place when the Spirit's convicting work through the Word meets a willing response in the human heart. The process is simple in outline but profound in reality.

On the day of Pentecost, Peter preached that Jesus is both Lord and Christ, attested by miracles, crucified by lawless hands, and raised by God. The crowd, hearing this, was "pierced to the heart" and asked, "What shall we do?" Peter answered,

Repent, and each of you be baptized in the name of Jesus Christ for the forgiveness of your sins, and you will receive the gift of the Holy Spirit.

The "piercing" was not a mysterious signal sent directly to their inner being apart from the sermon. It was the Spirit working through the very words Peter spoke. The evidence he presented, the Scriptures he quoted, and the conclusion he announced were all Spirit-given. When those truths cut through their defenses, that was the Spirit's influence, operating through rational conviction.

Their repentance and baptism were acts of obedience to the message. The "gift of the Holy Spirit" promised in that context is not a personal indwelling but the total package of blessings the Spirit would now make available through the new covenant—chiefly the forgiveness of sins, membership in the new people of God, and the hope of resurrection life guaranteed by the Spirit's past work in raising Jesus. These blessings are enjoyed by all who respond to the gospel in the same way, even though the temporary sign gifts that accompanied the earliest conversions have passed away.

In every genuine conversion today, the pattern is the same. Someone hears or reads the biblical message about Christ. The Spirit uses that message to expose sin, reveal the way of salvation, and press the urgency of response. If the person repents and obeys, it is because he has been persuaded and moved by that Spirit-inspired Word. If he refuses, it is because he hardens his heart against that same Word. In neither case has the Spirit bypassed the mind or overridden the will.

The Spirit's Indirect Operation, Never Apart from the Word

Because Scripture insists that faith comes by hearing the Word, we must reject the idea that the Holy Spirit operates directly on the heart in some separate, additional way. He does not secretly regenerate a person first and then later bring him to faith, as some systems claim. Nor does He give a mystical "inner light" that is independent of Scripture.

The Spirit's operation in conversion and sanctification is always **indirect** in the sense that it is carried out through the means of the Word. That does not mean His work is weak or uncertain. On the contrary, because He is God, the Word He has produced is living, penetrating, and powerful. But the power lies in the truth communicated, not in a hidden force working alongside the truth.

This understanding also protects us from confusing the Spirit's work with emotional experiences. People may feel stirred, fearful, joyful, or relieved when they encounter the gospel. These feelings are not wrong in themselves. Yet they are not the measure of the Spirit's presence. The true measure is whether the person submits to the doctrine the Spirit has revealed. A man may tremble like Felix and still refuse to repent. Another may respond with quiet determination and be truly converted. The Spirit's work is judged by obedience to the Word, not by intensity of sensation.

The Spirit's Continuing Work in Believers

Although this chapter focuses on the Spirit's relationship to the world, we must briefly note that He continues to work in those who have already believed—but still through the same instrument, the Word of God.

Believers are exhorted not to be drunk with wine but to be "filled with the Spirit." A parallel passage tells us to let the "word of Christ dwell in you richly." The two descriptions explain each other. To be filled with the Spirit is to be filled with the Word the Spirit has given, so that our thoughts, words, and songs are shaped by Scripture. It is not a special, second experience of inner indwelling; it is a life saturated with the Bible.

The Spirit's role in sanctification follows the same pattern. God has chosen believers for salvation "through sanctification by the Spirit and faith in the truth." The Spirit sets people apart for God by bringing them to believe the truth and by using that truth to renew their minds. When believers refuse to be conformed to this world but are transformed by the renewing of their minds, it happens through the message the Spirit has put into Scripture.

Romans 8:16 is sometimes quoted to support the idea of a mystical inner testimony. It says,

The Spirit himself testifies with our spirit that we are children of God.

This testimony is not a whisper in the heart. The Spirit "testifies" through the gospel—through the objective promises and descriptions in the Word. Our own spirit, that is, our renewed inner self, responds in agreement as we see that our faith, repentance, and obedience match what Scripture describes as the marks of a child of God. The

Spirit's testimony and our spirit's testimony meet in the same place: the written Word. Assurance is therefore grounded not in changing feelings but in the unchanging promises of God.

The Spirit, the World's Evil, and Human Responsibility

A proper view of the Spirit's work also clarifies why the world is as it is. Many people blame God for the evil they see, as if He were sending disasters to test or refine them or as if the Spirit were manipulating events to make life hard. Scripture rejects that idea completely.

Jehovah does not tempt with evil and does not try anyone by sending wicked circumstances. Troubles, injustices, and tragedies come from human imperfection, human sin, Satan, and the corrupted state of the world, not from God's hand. The Holy Spirit's role is not to design such hardships but to speak into them by means of the Word, showing what is truly wrong, calling people to repentance, and offering hope in Christ.

Human beings remain responsible for their choices. When they ignore or reject the Spirit's testimony in Scripture, they bear the blame for the consequences. God's foreknowledge of events does not cause those events; it reflects His perfect understanding of what free creatures will do. The Spirit's convicting work removes every excuse by making the truth known clearly.

This means that the world is not waiting for a new outpouring of mystical power. It is waiting for believers to proclaim the already-given Word, through which the Holy Spirit continues to confront and invite.

The Holy Spirit and the World Today

When we gather all these strands together, a clear picture emerges. The Holy Spirit is not absent from the world. He is powerfully at work, but He has bound Himself to a specific instrument—the Bible. Through that written Word He convicts the world of sin, righteousness, and judgment. He reveals the only way of salvation in Jesus Christ. He calls all people everywhere to repent. He brings about genuine conversion when people believe and obey the gospel. He continues to shape and assure believers by the same Word, producing holiness of life and steadfast hope.

He does all of this without indwelling anyone as a personal resident and without sending hardships to test anyone's faith. His operations are moral, rational, and scriptural. Wherever the Bible is opened with honesty, explained with accuracy, and believed with submission, there the Holy Spirit is working in this present age.

The Spirit and the world, then, are not connected by vague feelings or unexplained impulses. They are connected by the sharp, living, two-edged sword of the Word of God. That Word is His chosen channel, and through it He will continue to act until the day when the risen Christ returns and the world He has so patiently confronted will face final judgment or everlasting life.

CHAPTER 8 The Holy Spirit and Christians

Many churchgoers talk about "having the Spirit," "feeling the Spirit," or "being led by the Spirit," but often they mean very different things by those phrases. Some imagine the Holy Spirit as an inner voice whispering decisions about jobs, houses, and daily choices. Others assume He dwells inside their bodies as a personal Resident, separate from the Bible, giving private insights and experiences. Still others are afraid to say much of anything, because the language around the Spirit has been so badly twisted by charismatic and mystical teaching.

Scripture gives a much clearer, simpler, and more solid picture. The Holy Spirit is absolutely essential to Christian life, but His work in believers today is **not** a mystical indwelling and **not** a stream of extra-biblical impressions. He leads, convicts, assures, and transforms by one chosen instrument: **the Spirit-inspired Word of God**. Christians are "spiritual" not because a divine Person has moved into their bodies, but because they submit to the truth the Spirit has revealed and preserved in Scripture.

In this chapter we will carefully distinguish between what the Bible actually says about the Holy Spirit and Christians, and what later traditions and emotional ideas have added. We will look at key passages that are often misused to support a literal indwelling, show how they fit perfectly with a Word-centered view of the Spirit's work, and then describe how the Spirit truly guides, assures, and sanctifies believers today.

The Presence and Guidance of the Holy Spirit

It is often said that a true Christian life must "begin, be carried on, and be completed by the Spirit of God." That statement can be entirely true or quite misleading, depending on what we mean. If we mean that everything from conversion to final glorification comes from the plan, power, and revelation that the Holy Spirit has given, then yes, our whole Christian life is the Spirit's work. But if we mean that the Spirit must literally move inside us as an extra influence alongside the Word, or that He personally guides us by inner whispers and feelings, then we have stepped beyond Scripture.

The Bible does say,

Do you not know that you are a temple of God and that the Spirit of God dwells in you?

At first glance, this sounds like personal indwelling. But we must notice two things. First, in that verse Paul is addressing the congregation at Corinth in the plural. "You" are a temple of God—as a collective body. He is not saying that each individual believer's body is separately a tiny temple; he is saying that the **congregation** is the place where God's presence is represented on earth. Second, "dwells in you" is covenantal language. Jehovah "dwelt" in the tabernacle and temple in the Old Testament, yet He did not literally fit inside a building. His presence there meant that His name, His worship, and His law were centered there.

In the same way, the Spirit "dwells" in a congregation when that congregation is governed by the Spirit's teaching, grounded in the gospel the Spirit revealed, and obedient to the Scriptures He inspired. He "dwells" in Christians when His Word shapes their thinking, their priorities, and their character. This is a matter of **authority and influence through truth**, not of literal spatial presence.

There is no literal indwelling of the Holy Spirit in Christians today. The New Testament never says that the Spirit moves into our bodies as a second occupant living beside our own human spirit. When it speaks of "dwelling" and "being in" believers, it uses the same kind of language it uses for "Christ in you," "the word in you," and "faith in you"—all of which clearly describe **conditions of relationship and control**, not layers of spiritual entities stacked inside a human chest.

The Christian, then, is led, guided, and strengthened by the Holy Spirit precisely as he or she is led, guided, and strengthened by the Spirit's Word. To be "Spirit-led" is to be **Bible-led**. Anything that bypasses or contradicts Scripture cannot be the Spirit's guidance.

How the Spirit Brings People to Faith

No one becomes a Christian apart from the work of the Holy Spirit. But again, we must ask **how** He works.

Jesus said that when the Helper came,

he will convict the world concerning sin and righteousness and judgment.

This conviction is not accomplished by a mystical beam shot into the heart apart from truth. It happens as the Spirit uses the message about Christ to confront the mind and conscience.

On the day of Pentecost, Peter preached Jesus crucified and risen, declared that God had made Him both Lord and Christ, and showed from the Scriptures that these events were foretold. The crowd was "pierced to the heart" and cried out, "What shall we do?" That piercing was the Spirit's work through the **preached Word**. No one in that crowd received a silent voice apart from Peter's sermon. The Spirit convicted as they **heard and understood** the message He inspired.

The same principle holds today. The Spirit does not regenerate someone secretly and then later help him understand. He uses the Word to expose sin, explain the cross, and call for repentance and faith. When a person responds with genuine trust and obedience, all the credit belongs to Jehovah and to the Spirit who gave the gospel. When a person refuses, all the blame belongs to the one who has rejected the Spirit's testimony in Scripture.

Faith comes from hearing, and hearing comes by the Word of Christ. That is the Spirit's chosen method. There is no separate, invisible operation alongside the Word that creates faith apart from the message itself.

The Holy Spirit and the Word in the Christian's Daily Life

Once a person has believed and obeyed the gospel, the Holy Spirit does not switch to a different method. He continues to work through the same instrument—the inspired Word—to guide, correct, and grow the believer.

All Scripture is "God-breathed" and profitable for teaching, for reproof, for correction, and for training in righteousness so that the man of God may be complete, fully equipped for every good work. If the Spirit-breathed Scriptures are sufficient to make the believer **complete** and equipped for **every** good work, then nothing more is needed. There is no gap that must be filled by an indwelling Spirit adding extra information or secret directions.

The Word of God is described as "living and active and sharper than any two-edged sword," penetrating to the depths of the inner person and judging the thoughts and intentions of the heart. When a believer reads Scripture and feels exposed, corrected, or comforted, that is not the result of a second work beside the text. It is the Spirit's own Word doing what the Spirit intended.

To say, then, that the Holy Spirit guides Christians is simply to say that He guides them **by means of the Bible**. He does not bypass the intellect or replace the need for study. Instead, He has given a book that requires careful reading, comparison, and meditation. As we come to understand that book correctly, using sound grammatical-historical principles, we are learning the very mind of the Spirit.

This is why Christians must beware of the phrase, "The Spirit told me..." when it is used to justify decisions that have no basis in Scripture or even contradict Scripture. The Spirit does not contradict

Himself. His voice is the voice of the Bible. To appeal to "the Spirit" in order to sidestep the plain teaching of Scripture is to blame the Spirit for our own desires.

Sanctification by the Spirit and the Truth

Sanctification means being set apart for Jehovah and being increasingly conformed to the image of Christ. This also is the Spirit's work—but again, not through mystical indwelling.

Paul writes that God chose believers "for salvation through sanctification by the Spirit and faith in the truth." Here the Spirit and "the truth" are side by side, not as two separate forces, but as cause and means. The Spirit sanctifies by bringing people to faith in the truth, and then by using that truth to renew their minds. Jesus prayed, "Sanctify them in the truth; your word is truth." That prayer explains the method: sanctification occurs as the Spirit's Word changes how we think, love, and choose.

Romans 12:2 urges believers not to be conformed to this age but to be transformed by the renewing of the mind. Renewing the mind is not a mystical feeling; it is a deep reorientation of thinking brought about by sustained exposure to the Spirit-inspired Scriptures. As the Word corrects our assumptions, reshapes our desires, and clarifies our priorities, we begin to act differently. That is the Spirit's sanctifying work.

Some people speak as though holiness comes mainly from "yielding" to inner impulses, waiting for the Spirit to move, or asking for a second blessing. The New Testament points in a different direction: it calls believers to fill their minds with the Word, to put sin to death by deliberate choices, to imitate Christ's example, and to encourage one another with sound teaching. The Spirit stands behind all of that, because He is the Author of the Word and the One who used the apostles to give us those commands and patterns.

There is no sanctification apart from Scripture. Any supposed "Spirit-led" holiness that neglects the Bible, downgrades doctrine, or treats obedience as unimportant is a counterfeit. True sanctification is "by the Spirit and faith in the truth."

The Witness of the Spirit and Christian Assurance

One of the most misused texts in discussions about the Holy Spirit and Christians is Romans 8:16:

The Spirit himself testifies with our spirit that we are children of God.

Many take this to mean that the Spirit whispers directly to the individual believer, "You are saved," apart from any reference to Scripture. This turns assurance into a subjective feeling and opens the door to chaos: two people can claim opposite things, both insisting, "The Spirit told me."

Paul's words can and must be understood in harmony with everything we have already seen. The Spirit "testifies" through the gospel He has revealed. In that gospel He describes who the children of God are, what they believe, how they live, and what promises they have. When we read those descriptions and promises, it is the Spirit speaking.

Our own spirit—that is, our renewed inner self, our conscience and understanding—"testifies with" His when we see that our faith and life match what the Spirit has said. For example, Scripture says that those who believe in Christ, repent of sin, confess His name, and are baptized into Him receive forgiveness and belong to Him. It says that those who walk according to the Spirit's teaching, not according to the flesh, are sons of God.

When a believer honestly examines himself in light of those passages and sees that, though imperfect, he truly fits that pattern, his own spirit agrees: "Yes, I am one of those described here." The Spirit's testimony in the Word and our spirit's testimony in our conscience line up, and assurance grows.

This is very different from a private voice. It is objective and testable. If someone claims assurance while stubbornly living in sin and disregarding Scripture, then his "inner peace" does not match the Spirit's testimony in the Word. In that case, the Spirit does **not** testify that such a person is a child of God, no matter what he feels.

Assurance comes from hearing what the Spirit has said in Scripture and then honestly comparing our lives to that standard. When there is agreement, we may rightly rejoice that He has confirmed our adoption through the gospel.

Walking by the Spirit and the Fruit of the Spirit

Galatians 5 gives another key picture of the Spirit's relationship to Christians. Paul says, "Walk by the Spirit, and you will not carry out the desire of the flesh." He then contrasts the "works of the flesh"—which include immorality, idolatry, strife, jealousy, fits of anger, drunkenness, and similar things—with the "fruit of the Spirit," which is love, joy, peace, patience, kindness, goodness, faithfulness, gentleness, and self-control.

To walk by the Spirit is not to drift along with inner nudges. It is to conduct life according to the teaching the Spirit has revealed. The Galatians had been hearing and obeying the gospel. Then false teachers arrived, urging them to adopt a different message. Paul calls them back to the pure teaching they first received and insists that living by that message is walking by the Spirit.

The fruit of the Spirit, likewise, is not a mystical substance. It is the character produced when a person's mind and heart are re-shaped by the Spirit's Word. Love grows as we see how Christ loved us and obey the command to love one another. Joy deepens as we trust the promises the Spirit has recorded. Peace develops as we learn from Scripture who God is and rest in His care. Patience, kindness, goodness, faithfulness, gentleness, and self-control all arise as we submit our attitudes and choices to what the Spirit has said.

People sometimes examine themselves for "fruit" while ignoring the means by which the Spirit produces that fruit. They want the qualities but neglect the book that cultivates them. The result is either discouragement ("I see so little fruit, so maybe I do not have the Spirit") or superficiality ("I feel loving and peaceful, so I must be Spirit-filled," even while ignoring obvious disobedience).

The right approach is to root ourselves deeply in the Spirit's Word, obey what we find there, and then recognize the changes He brings about as His fruit. The focus remains on Scripture and obedience, not on chasing feelings.

Spiritual Gifts Then and Now

The Holy Spirit also gave "gifts" to Christians, especially in the first century. We must, however, distinguish between **miraculous gifts tied to the apostolic age** and the ongoing abilities and responsibilities believers have today.

In the early congregations, the Spirit granted gifts such as prophecy, tongues, interpretation, miracles, healings, and special knowledge. These were manifestations of the Spirit that confirmed the new revelation, guided congregations before the New Testament was complete, and demonstrated that the same God was at work among Jews and Gentiles. These gifts were not distributed randomly; they often came through the laying on of the apostles' hands and were concentrated in that transitional period.

Once the New Testament was complete and the last apostle died, those miraculous gifts no longer had a purpose. The revelation they supported was now written down and preserved. The Spirit had finished speaking in that way. Today we do not expect tongues, prophecy, or healing gifts as normal features of church life. Claims to such gifts usually rest on misunderstanding, emotional pressure, or even deliberate deceit.

This does not mean Christians have no "gifts" now. The New Testament also speaks of abilities and roles such as teaching, serving, encouraging, giving generously, leading diligently, and showing mercy. These are not supernatural powers in the sense of bypassing natural capacities. Rather, they are the ways believers use their God-given abilities in obedience to Scripture for the building up of the body. The Spirit stands behind such gifts in the sense that He has prescribed them in the Word and uses them to strengthen His people. But He does not infuse them as mysterious forces.

When a Christian teaches faithfully from Scripture, visits the sick, encourages the discouraged, or manages resources honestly for the congregation, he or she is using "gifts" in a biblical sense. These are Spirit-directed because they follow patterns and instructions the Spirit has given in the New Testament.

"Led by the Spirit" in the Christian Life

Many Christians use the phrase "led by the Spirit" to describe almost any decision they feel deeply about. But Scripture uses that phrase in a far more specific way.

Romans 8:14 says, "For all who are being led by the Spirit of God, these are sons of God." Some take this to mean that only those who follow an inner guidance system are really God's children. But in the context of Romans 8, being "led by the Spirit" stands in contrast to living "according to the flesh." The flesh represents sinful desires, worldly patterns of thinking, and resistance to God's revealed will. The Spirit represents the teaching and guidance He has given in the gospel.

To be led by the Spirit, therefore, is to let the Spirit's Word direct our choices instead of letting sinful impulses rule. It is highly practical: refusing sexual immorality because the Spirit condemns it, rejecting bitterness because the Spirit commands forgiveness, telling the truth because the Spirit forbids lying, and so on. The Spirit "leads" by telling us plainly in Scripture what pleases God and what does not.

This protects us from two serious mistakes. One is trusting our feelings and calling that "the Spirit," which can lead to disobedience cloaked in pious language. The other is reducing Christian guidance to bare human wisdom, as if the Spirit had nothing to do with our daily decisions. The truth is that He leads us whenever we submit our decisions to the principles and commands of His Word. The more we know that Word, the more clearly we can see how to act in each situation.

Edward D. Andrews

The Comfort and Help of the Spirit

Jesus called the Spirit the "Helper" and promised that He would be with His followers forever. He spoke of the Spirit as the One who would teach, remind, testify, and glorify Christ. For the apostles, this meant direct revelation and supernatural recall of Jesus' words. For us, it means that the Spirit has preserved those teachings in Scripture and continues to use them to comfort and strengthen believers.

The comfort of the Holy Spirit does not come as unexplained waves of calm descending out of nowhere. It comes as the truths He has revealed sink into the heart. When a believer facing grief recalls that nothing can separate him from the love of God in Christ, that is the Spirit comforting through Romans 8. When someone struggling with guilt embraces the promise that if we confess our sins Jehovah is faithful and righteous to forgive, that is the Spirit comforting through that verse. When a weary Christian remembers that our present sufferings are not worth comparing with the glory to be revealed, that is the Spirit lifting the heart through the Scriptures He breathed out.

The Spirit is our Helper and Advocate because He has given us a perfect Word and because He stands behind that Word as we read, hear, and speak it. He does not need to bypass the Scriptures to comfort us. He comforts us most deeply by pressing Scripture into our minds and hearts until we truly believe what we read.

Christians and the Spirit Today

When we pull all of this together, the picture is both humbling and liberating. Christians today are not half-equipped compared to first-century believers. We are not waiting for a second blessing, a personal indwelling, or a fresh descent of power. We already possess the completed revelation that the Holy Spirit gave through prophets and apostles. He now works through that revelation, and it is sufficient.

There is no literal indwelling of the Holy Spirit in the believer. There is no direct mystical influence on the heart apart from the Word. There is no divine testing through hardships sent from God. Instead, there is a living, sharp, Spirit-breathed Bible and a world full of people whose greatest need is to hear and obey it.

A Christian who reads Scripture carefully, interprets it with sound, conservative methods, believes it with all his heart, and obeys it in daily life is a Christian truly walking by the Spirit. He may never feel anything dramatic, but his life will be marked by growing holiness, deeper assurance, and steady usefulness to others. That is the real work of the Holy Spirit in Christians today—quiet, powerful, and entirely tied to the Word He has given.

Edward D. Andrews

CHAPTER 9 The Work of the Holy Spirit

When Christians ask, "What is the Holy Spirit doing today?" they often expect an answer about inner feelings, sudden impressions, and invisible movements within the heart. Others look back at the first century and assume that if tongues, prophecies, and miracles are not happening, then the Spirit must be largely absent. Both views overlook what Scripture actually teaches. The Bible gives a rich, ordered picture of the Spirit's work—from creation, through the prophets and apostles, to the finished Scriptures and the life of the church. That work is vast, but it is never vague. It is powerful, but it is never mystical in the way modern religious talk imagines.

In particular, we must be very clear about two truths that this book has emphasized: first, **there is no literal indwelling of the Holy**

Spirit in Christians today; and second, **the Holy Spirit now works entirely through the Spirit-inspired Word of God,** not by bypassing the mind with secret influences. Passages that speak of the Spirit "dwelling in" believers, including Romans 8:11, can and must be understood in this Word-centered way.

This chapter will survey the work of the Holy Spirit across Scripture and then draw together how He operates now—in the world, in conversion, in sanctification, and in the ongoing life and service of Christians.

The Work of the Holy Spirit in the Old Testament

The first verses of the Bible already show the Spirit at work. Genesis describes the earth as without form and empty, with darkness over the surface of the deep, and "the Spirit of God" moving over the waters. Here the Spirit is the divine power bringing order out of chaos, preparing the world for the stages of creation that follow. He is not an impersonal force but the active presence of Jehovah shaping the universe.

Throughout the Old Testament, the Spirit acts in at least three major ways.

First, He is the life-giver and sustainer. Psalm 104 says that when God hides His face, creatures are troubled; when He takes away their breath, they die and return to dust; when He sends forth His Spirit, they are created, and He renews the face of the ground. Job can say, "The Spirit of God has made me, and the breath of the Almighty gives me life." Our very existence is dependent on the Spirit's ongoing work.

Second, He empowers individuals for particular tasks. The judges who delivered Israel—Othniel, Gideon, Jephthah, and

Samson—are each described as having the Spirit of Jehovah come upon them. This does not mean the Spirit moved into their hearts as a permanent inner guest. It means that He clothed them with power for specific acts of leadership and deliverance. Their moral failings make it obvious that task-empowerment is not the same as inner sanctification.

The same pattern appears with kings and craftsmen. Saul is told that the Spirit will come upon him and he will prophesy, confirming his appointment as king. When he persists in disobedience, the Spirit of Jehovah departs from him. David is anointed, and the Spirit comes mightily upon him from that day forward. Bezalel is "filled with the Spirit of God" in wisdom and skill for constructing the tabernacle. Again, the language focuses on equipping for roles in God's plan, not on a universal, inner indwelling.

Third, the Spirit is the Author of revelation. The prophets speak as they are carried along by the Spirit. Nehemiah says Jehovah admonished Israel "by your Spirit through your prophets." Zechariah recalls that the people "made their hearts like flint so that they could not hear the law and the words which Jehovah of hosts had sent by his Spirit through the former prophets." Isaiah laments that Israel "grieved his holy Spirit." In each case, the Spirit's work is tied to words—to messages delivered, written, and rejected or obeyed.

The Old Testament therefore presents the Spirit as Creator, Sustainer, Empowerer, and Revealer. But it never portrays ordinary believers as having a literal, constant, personal indwelling of the Spirit. Their experience of the Spirit is **mediated through the Word He gives** and the leaders He empowers.

The Work of the Holy Spirit in the New Testament

When we move into the New Testament, the Spirit's role becomes even more focused on Christ and the spread of the gospel. He is involved at each key stage of redemption history.

He is active in the conception of Jesus, as the angel tells Mary that the Holy Spirit will come upon her and the power of the Most High will overshadow her. He is present at Jesus' baptism, descending like a dove as the Father's voice declares the Son's identity. Jesus reads the prophecy, "The Spirit of the Lord Jehovah is upon me," and announces that this is fulfilled in His ministry.

The Spirit is involved in the resurrection of Jesus. Romans 8:11 calls Him "the Spirit of him who raised Jesus from the dead." That act stands at the center of Christian hope: Jehovah, by His Spirit, raised the crucified Jesus and thereby confirmed that He is indeed Lord and Christ.

At Pentecost, the Spirit is poured out in a unique way, marking the beginning of the apostolic church. The apostles speak in real foreign languages they had not studied, bearing witness to the mighty works of God. Peter explains that Jesus, having been exalted to the right hand of God, has "poured out this that you yourselves are seeing and hearing."

It is crucial to understand that this cluster of events—Christ's anointing, the apostles' empowerment, and the miraculous gifts distributed in the earliest churches—belongs to the **foundational stage** of the Christian faith. The Spirit is still the same today, but His mode of operation has changed because His plan has moved from **giving** revelation to **preserving and applying** revelation.

Edward D. Andrews

He no longer produces new Scripture. He no longer gives prophets and apostles fresh messages that add to the Bible. He no longer confirms such new messages with miraculous gifts scattered across congregations. Those things were temporary, "partial" provisions until the "perfect"—the complete New Testament—was in place. Now His work centers on the Scriptures themselves.

The Holy Spirit's Work of Conviction

Jesus described one major strand of the Spirit's work when He said that the Helper would "convict the world concerning sin and righteousness and judgment." This description does not portray a mystical inner feeling that descends on people apart from truth. It describes what happens when the Spirit uses the gospel to confront the world.

He convicts concerning sin "because they do not believe in" Christ. The greatest sin is unbelief—a refusal to respond to the clear testimony that the Spirit has given about the Son. The Spirit exposes this sin whenever the gospel is preached or read. At Pentecost, when Peter declares that the crowd has crucified the One whom God has made Lord and Christ, their being "pierced to the heart" is the Spirit's conviction working through his sermon.

He convicts concerning righteousness "because I go to the Father and you no longer see me." Jesus' resurrection and exaltation demonstrate that Jehovah has declared Him righteous and accepted His sacrifice. The Spirit points to that fact through the apostolic message. The world's standards of righteousness crumble when measured against the righteousness revealed in Christ.

He convicts concerning judgment "because the ruler of this world has been judged." The cross and resurrection are also a judicial

134

sentence on Satan. The Spirit announces that the ruler of this world stands condemned and that those who persist in following his rebellion will share his fate.

All of this happens **through the Word**. The Spirit convicts by bringing people face to face with the facts, promises, and warnings recorded in Scripture. There is no separate, invisible operation parallel to the Word. His convicting power lies precisely in the sharp, clear truths He has caused to be written.

Regeneration and New Life by the Spirit Through the Word

The Bible also speaks of the Spirit's work in "regeneration"—the granting of new life. Titus 3:5 says that God saved us, not on the basis of deeds we have done in righteousness, but according to His mercy, by the washing of regeneration and renewing by the Holy Spirit. This renewing is not a mystical sensation apart from the gospel. It is the new life that comes when a person, convicted by the Spirit's message, responds with repentance and faith.

Peter explains that believers have been born again "not of perishable seed but of imperishable, through the living and enduring word of God." The Word is the instrument the Spirit uses to bring about this new birth. When the good news about Jesus is preached, the Spirit is active in that message, and those who receive it in obedient faith are "made alive" together with Christ.

Regeneration is therefore not a secret act in which the Spirit enters the heart of an unbeliever directly, apart from the mind and the message. It is His work **through** the message. The gospel is "the power of God for salvation" because the Spirit has loaded it with His own authority and truth.

The same understanding applies to Romans 8:11, a verse often pressed into service for the doctrine of literal indwelling:

If the Spirit of him who raised Jesus from the dead dwells in you, he who raised Christ Jesus from the dead will also give life to your mortal bodies through his Spirit who dwells in you.

Read in context, this verse has nothing to do with a personal, metaphysical indwelling of the Spirit in believers' bodies. Paul has just contrasted those who are "according to the flesh" with those who are "according to the Spirit." To be "in the Spirit" is to belong to the realm where the Spirit's resurrection truth and authority hold sway. The Spirit of the One who raised Jesus is said to "dwell in you" because believers have embraced the Spirit's message, now live under the Spirit's revealed will, and stand within the group that the Spirit has marked out as belonging to Christ.

The promise that God will "also give life to your mortal bodies" looks forward to the future resurrection. Just as the Spirit raised Jesus, so He guarantees that those who belong to Christ will one day be raised bodily. The basis of that hope is not an inner occupant that keeps working from the inside, but the objective fact of Christ's resurrection and the Spirit's promise recorded in Scripture.

Romans 8:11, then, is about **resurrection certainty through the Spirit's past work in Christ and His present authority over believers by the gospel.** It does not teach, and cannot be stretched to teach, that the Spirit literally lives inside Christians as a second Person in their bodies.

The Holy Spirit's Work in Sanctification

Sanctification is the lifelong process by which believers are set apart for Jehovah and increasingly conformed to the image of Christ.

Scripture attributes this work to the Holy Spirit but always links it to the truth He has revealed.

Paul gives thanks that God chose the Thessalonian believers "for salvation through sanctification by the Spirit and faith in the truth." Sanctification happens in the sphere of "faith in the truth"—not apart from it. The Spirit's role is to use that truth to reshape the believer's thinking, desires, and actions.

Jesus prayed, "Sanctify them in the truth; your word is truth." He did not ask for a vague, inner experience. He asked that His followers be set apart by the truth of God's Word. This prayer is answered as the Spirit takes the written Word and makes it effective in those who read and obey it.

Romans 12:2 urges believers not to be conformed to this age but to be transformed by the renewing of their mind. That renewal comes as the Spirit's Word replaces worldly patterns of thought with biblical patterns. This is a real change, but it is not magical. It is the fruit of sustained, humble engagement with Scripture and concrete obedience.

When Galatians 5 speaks of the "fruit of the Spirit"—love, joy, peace, patience, kindness, goodness, faithfulness, gentleness, self-control—it is describing the character that emerges when a life is governed by the Spirit's teaching. Walking by the Spirit means living in step with the truth He has revealed. The fruit is His because the pattern comes from Him and the power comes from His Word.

None of this requires the Spirit to indwell believers as an internal Residence. It requires Him to have spoken, and requires believers to listen. That is exactly what we have: a completed Bible and the responsibility to receive it as the Spirit's voice.

The Holy Spirit's Work in Empowering Service

The Spirit also empowers believers for service. Acts 1:8 records Jesus' promise to the apostles that they would receive power when the Holy Spirit came upon them and that they would be His witnesses to the ends of the earth. In that setting, the power included miraculous gifts and extraordinary courage, because they were launching the gospel into a hostile world without a completed New Testament.

In the apostolic churches, the Spirit granted gifts for building up the body. Some of these gifts—prophecy, tongues, miracles, healings—were obviously supernatural. Others—teaching, leading, encouraging—worked largely through ordinary human abilities directed by Scripture. All of them were "manifestations of the Spirit" because He Himself designed and distributed them.

The miraculous gifts were temporary. They confirmed new revelation and guided congregations before the New Testament was complete. Once the canon was closed and the last apostle died, the Spirit no longer needed to supply such signs. The foundation had been laid.

Today the Spirit continues to empower service, but He does so by giving light through Scripture, by shaping the character of believers through that same Scripture, and by prescribing roles and responsibilities that match the abilities God has given. When a Christian teaches the Bible faithfully, visits the sick, encourages the discouraged, leads with integrity, or supports the work generously, that service is "in the Spirit" because it follows the patterns and commands He has put in the Word.

The power He gives is not a mysterious force passing from hand to hand. It is the moral and spiritual strength that comes from trusting the promises He has recorded and obeying the duties He has revealed.

The Holy Spirit as Comforter and Advocate

Jesus called the Spirit "another Helper" and promised that He would be with the apostles forever. He told them that the Spirit would teach them all things, bring to their remembrance all He had said, testify about Him, and guide them into all the truth. Those promises were fulfilled in the apostolic age when the Spirit gave them infallible understanding and caused them to write the New Testament.

For believers today, the comfort and help of the Spirit comes through those very apostolic writings. The Spirit still teaches, but He does so by means of a completed Bible. He still reminds, but He reminds us of what is written. He still testifies about Christ, but He does so by shining the light of Scripture into our minds, not by adding new revelations.

When a believer under pressure recalls that nothing can separate him from the love of God in Christ, that assurance is the comfort of the Spirit through Romans 8. When someone burdened with guilt clings to the promise that if we confess our sins God is faithful and righteous to forgive, the Spirit is advocating for that believer through the written Word. When a suffering Christian endures by fixing his hope on the resurrection and the new creation, the Spirit is strengthening him through the passages He inspired about those realities.

The Spirit is truly the Comforter and Advocate, but His help is objective and Word-centered, not mystical and feeling-centered.

What the Holy Spirit Does Not Do

To avoid confusion, it is helpful to state plainly what the Holy Spirit **does not** do in this age.

He does not indwell believers literally. The language of "dwelling" and "being in" Christians is relational and covenantal, describing the Spirit's ownership and influence through the Word, not a second Person living inside the body.

He does not give new revelation. The faith has been "once for all delivered to the holy ones." The canon is closed. Any claim to Spirit-given messages beyond Scripture must be rejected.

He does not bypass the Word to guide by private impressions. The Spirit's guidance is exercised through the clear teaching and principles of Scripture. We are led by the Spirit when we submit our decisions to that teaching.

He does not test believers by sending evil or hardships. Trials arise from human imperfection, a fallen world, and the malice of Satan and demons—not from God. The Spirit's role in suffering is to comfort and strengthen through the Word, never to design calamity.

He does not override human freedom. The Spirit calls, convicts, and pleads through Scripture, but He does not force anyone into belief or obedience. Those who reject His message are responsible for that rejection.

Understanding what the Holy Spirit does **not** do helps us appreciate more fully what He **does** do: speak once for all through Scripture and then work through that Scripture to bring people to salvation, transform their lives, equip them for service, and sustain their hope.

The work of the Holy Spirit, then, is anything but small. It spans creation, revelation, redemption, conviction, regeneration, sanctification, empowerment, and comfort. But it is always anchored in His Word. In this age He has chosen to operate **only** through that Word. To hear the Bible rightly is to hear the Spirit Himself. To obey it is to walk by the Spirit. To trust its promises is to rest in the Spirit's work. Nothing more mystical, and nothing less powerful, is needed.

CHAPTER 10 How Are We to Understand the Indwelling of the Holy Spirit?

Talk about the "indwelling of the Holy Spirit" and you quickly discover that many Christians are using the same words but meaning very different things. Some imagine the Holy Spirit literally living inside their physical bodies as a kind of inner Guest who gives them secret impressions and feelings. Others think of indwelling as a second, deeper experience that comes after conversion. Still others simply repeat phrases they have heard without ever examining the passages behind them.

If we are going to write about the Holy Spirit with accuracy and reverence, we must ask a very direct question: **What does Scripture** itself mean when it speaks of the Spirit being "in" believers or "dwelling" in them? Does it teach a literal, personal, spatial indwelling, or is it using relational and covenant language to describe the Spirit's authority and influence through the Word He has given?

This chapter will show that the Bible does **not** teach a literal indwelling of the Holy Spirit in Christians. The Spirit does not move into our bodies as a second Person living side by side with our own human spirit. Instead, He "dwells" in believers and in the church as He rules, shapes, and owns them through the Spirit-inspired Scriptures. We will examine the key texts used to defend a literal indwelling, set them back into their contexts, and see that they fit perfectly with a Word-centered understanding of the Spirit's work.

What People Commonly Mean by "Indwelling"

Before turning to the passages, it helps to clarify the popular views.

Many Calvinistic writers speak of the Spirit indwelling believers in order to regenerate them, give them faith, and keep them saved. In this view, the Spirit must enter the person first so that he can even respond to the gospel. The Spirit's supposed inner residency becomes the explanation for faith, repentance, obedience, and perseverance.

Charismatic and Pentecostal circles often add another layer. For them, "having the Spirit" or "receiving the Spirit" frequently refers to an experience of power after conversion, marked by tongues, prophecies, or strong emotions. Indwelling becomes almost identical with felt spiritual excitement.

In ordinary church talk, many Christians simply assume that when they felt strongly moved at some point, that feeling was "the Holy Spirit in me." The Spirit becomes a way of naming our strongest inner impressions, whether or not those impressions are grounded in Scripture.

None of these ideas comes from careful exegesis. They rest on reading modern assumptions back into a handful of phrases—"dwells in you," "in your hearts," "in you"—without asking whether the Bible itself ever uses similar language for things that are clearly **not** literal or mystical.

Scripture speaks of the word of Christ dwelling in believers, of the gospel abiding in them, of faith and love being in them, and of Christ Himself living in their hearts. No one imagines that the letters on the page are physically inside the chest or that Christ is located spatially beneath the ribs. We instinctively understand those expressions to describe relationship, control, and influence. We must allow the same kind of language when we read about the Holy Spirit.

Covenant Presence: How God "Dwells" with His People

The Old Testament gives us the background for all New Testament "dwelling" language. Jehovah repeatedly says that He will "dwell" among His people and that they will be His people and He will be their God. He places His name in the tabernacle and later in the temple. His glory fills those places.

Yet the same Scriptures insist that the heavens, even the highest heaven, cannot contain Him, much less a house made by human hands. His "dwelling" in the tabernacle or temple does not mean that His essence is confined to a building. It means that He has chosen to make His presence known there, to meet with His people there, and to have His worship and law centered there. His dwelling is covenantal and representational, not spatial.

This is the pattern carried over into the New Testament. When the church is called a temple, the point is not that God has squeezed Himself into our meeting place. The point is that Jehovah has taken up His covenant presence among a people shaped by the gospel, just as He once took up His covenant presence in the tabernacle and temple.

With that background in mind, we can approach the "indwelling" passages with much more clarity.

Romans 8:9-11: In the Spirit, Not in the Flesh

Romans chapter 8 is one of the main battlegrounds for debates about indwelling. Verses 9–11 are especially quoted:

However, you are not in the flesh but in the Spirit, if indeed the Spirit of God dwells in you. But if anyone does not have the Spirit of Christ, he does not belong to him. If Christ is in you, though the body is dead because of sin, yet the spirit is life because of righteousness. But if the Spirit of him who raised Jesus from the dead dwells in you, he who raised Christ Jesus from the dead will also give life to your mortal bodies through his Spirit who dwells in you.

At first glance, the repeated "dwells in you" and the parallel "Christ is in you" might sound like literal residency. But the context gives a different picture.

Paul has been contrasting two realms: "flesh" and "Spirit." To be "in the flesh" is to be under the rule of sin, following desires and patterns that are hostile to God. To be "in the Spirit" is to be under the rule of the Spirit's revelation in the gospel, reconciled to God through Christ, and walking according to His will. These are legal and moral spheres, not locations in the body.

When Paul says "the Spirit of God dwells in you," he is saying that believers belong to the realm where the Spirit's message and authority hold sway. The Spirit "dwells" in them the way a king "dwells" in his kingdom—as the One whose rule defines their identity. The next line makes this explicit: "If anyone does not have the Spirit of Christ, he does not belong to him." Having the Spirit here means belonging to Christ, not harboring a second Person inside the chest.

Notice too that Paul freely shifts language: the Spirit of God dwells in you; you have the Spirit of Christ; Christ is in you. If we insisted on a literal idea for each phrase, we would have to imagine both Christ and the Spirit occupying the same physical interior space. It is obvious that Paul is speaking about relationship and allegiance. The same logic that makes "Christ in you" non-literal should be applied to "the Spirit in you."

Verse 11, often used to defend indwelling, actually strengthens this point. Paul describes the Spirit as "the Spirit of him who raised Jesus from the dead" and then promises that God will give life to our mortal bodies "through his Spirit who dwells in you." The emphasis is on resurrection hope. The Spirit who raised Jesus guarantees that those who belong to Christ will also be raised.

The Spirit "dwells in you" in the sense that His resurrection power and promise define your destiny. Because you stand within the sphere where His gospel has been believed and obeyed, your future bodily life is as secure as Christ's. Romans 8:11 is not a prooftext for a mystical inner presence; it is a promise that the same Spirit who raised Jesus will one day raise all who are united to Him by obedient faith.

This is why earlier chapters in this book have repeatedly appealed to Romans 8:11. The verse is central for resurrection hope, not for a doctrine of literal indwelling.

The Temple Texts: 1 Corinthians 3:16-17 and 1 Corinthians 6:19-20

Another group of passages often cited speak of believers as a "temple" of the Holy Spirit.

In 1 Corinthians 3:16–17 Paul asks,

Do you not know that you are a temple of God and that the Spirit of God dwells in you?

Here the "you" is plural. Paul is addressing the congregation as a whole. The Corinthian church has been torn by factions, with different groups rallying around different preachers. Paul reminds them that they are not separate clubs but one temple. To damage that unity is to damage God's temple, and God takes that very seriously.

The temple imagery points back to the Old Testament. The Spirit of God "dwelt" in Israel's midst as He owned, directed, and protected them through His Word, His priests, and His appointed worship. In the same way, the Spirit "dwells" in the congregation at Corinth because this is the community shaped by the gospel He inspired. Their status as a temple depends on their faithfulness to that message, not on a mysterious internal presence.

In 1 Corinthians 6:19–20 Paul turns to sexual immorality and writes,

Or do you not know that your body is a temple of the Holy Spirit who is in you, whom you have from God, and that you are not your own? For you were bought with a price. Therefore glorify God in your body.

Here the "you" is singular, and the misuse of the physical body is in view. Some have concluded that this must teach literal indwelling. But notice Paul's actual argument.

147

First, he has just said that believers are joined to Christ. The body is for the Lord, and the Lord is for the body. To unite the body to sin is to drag what belongs to Christ into defilement.

Second, he reminds them that they have been "bought with a price." The imagery is from the slave market. They are owned by Christ because He paid for them with His blood.

Third, he uses the temple language. A temple is a place set apart, reserved for sacred use. If your body is a temple of the Holy Spirit "whom you have from God," that means your whole physical life is set apart for the Spirit's purpose. You are not free to use it as you please.

The focus is on ownership and consecration, not on spatial residency. The Spirit is "in" these believers because His authoritative Word has claimed them, because the gospel has marked them out as belonging to Jehovah, and because their bodies are now instruments of service rather than tools of sin. To "glorify God in your body" is to obey the Spirit's commands with your hands, eyes, and feet.

If the phrase "in you" here had to mean a literal occupant, then "Christ in you" and "faith in you" would also have to be literal. But no one reads those expressions that way.

The Upper Room Promises: John 14-16

Two passages from the Upper Room discourse are often appealed to in discussions of indwelling and inner guidance:

I will ask the Father, and He will give you another Helper, that He may be with you forever; that is the Spirit of truth... you know him because he abides with you and will be in you. (John 14:16–17)

But when he, the Spirit of truth, comes, he will guide you into all the truth. (John 16:13)

Many sermons and books apply these promises directly to every Christian, as though Jesus were saying that the Spirit would personally indwell and individually guide each believer into "all the truth" through private impressions. This is a serious interpretive error.

In context, Jesus is speaking to the apostles on the night before His execution. He is preparing them for their unique role as foundational witnesses and authors of the New Testament. The Helper He promises will teach **them** all things and bring **to their remembrance** all that He said. That is inspiration language. The apostles will be able to recall and record Jesus' teaching accurately because the Spirit will be with them in that task.

When Jesus says the Spirit "abides with you and will be in you," He is looking ahead to Pentecost, when the Helper will come in power upon that apostolic band and launch the new phase of redemptive history. The promise that the Spirit will "guide you into all the truth" is fulfilled when the apostles receive, proclaim, and write the full message of the gospel.

Christians today do benefit from these promises, but **indirectly.** We enjoy the results of the Spirit's guidance of the apostles every time we read the New Testament. We have access to "all the truth" because the Spirit has already given it through the apostolic writings. We do not need, and are not promised, a fresh inner voice. We need to listen to what has already been said.

To use John 14:16–17 and John 16:13 to defend a private, mystical indwelling and individual infallible guidance is to take promises given to the apostles for their foundational work and rip them out of their historical setting.

John 7:37–39: Rivers of Living Water

Another famous passage says that whoever believes in Christ will have "rivers of living water" flowing from within. John immediately explains,

This he said about the Spirit, whom those who believed in him were to receive, for as yet the Spirit had not been given, because Jesus was not yet glorified.

Some interpret this to mean that every believer in all ages has a personal inner spring of the Spirit flooding out in ecstatic experiences. But once again we must read the text in its historical place.

John tells us that Jesus spoke these words before the glorification, that is, before His death, resurrection, and ascension. The "giving" of the Spirit in view here is the great Pentecost event and its extension to Gentiles. The rivers of living water describe the powerful, outward, life-giving effect of the gospel when the Spirit empowers its proclamation.

Those who believed in Christ in that first generation did indeed become channels of living water. The Spirit used their preaching, their writings, and their faithful lives to bring others to salvation. Today we participate in the same stream when we teach and live according to the completed Scriptures. But none of this requires or implies a second Person literally gushing inside our physical bodies.

Galatians 4:6 and Ephesians 3:16–17: Spirit and Christ in the Heart

Two other passages are often brought forward:

Because you are sons, God has sent the Spirit of his Son into our hearts, crying, "Abba! Father!" (Galatians 4:6)

...that he would grant you, according to the riches of his glory, to be strengthened with power through his Spirit in the inner man, so that Christ may dwell in your hearts through faith. (Ephesians 3:16–17)

In Galatians, the point is adoption. Those who have believed the gospel are no longer slaves under the law but sons and heirs. The Spirit of God's Son is "sent into our hearts" in the sense that the message of sonship and the confidence to cry "Abba, Father" take root at the very center of our being. We no longer fear God as a distant Judge but come to Him as Father because the Spirit's gospel has convinced us that we belong to Him.

Ephesians explicitly states that Christ dwells in hearts "through faith." The means of His dwelling is not mystical occupancy but trust in the truths revealed by the Spirit. As believers grasp the breadth and length and height and depth of Christ's love through the Word, their inner lives become more and more filled with Him.

If "Christ dwelling in hearts through faith" is non-literal, then "Spirit in our hearts" must be understood the same way. Both phrases describe the deep, controlling influence of the Word. The heart is the seat of thought, desire, and will. To have the Spirit or Christ in the heart is to have their teaching and their lordship governing that inner life.

The Mind of Christ and the So-Called "Illumination" Text

Some argue that the Holy Spirit must personally indwell believers in order to help them understand Scripture. They appeal especially to 1 Corinthians 2:12–14, where Paul says that we have received the Spirit from God so that we may know the things freely given to us, and that the natural man does not accept the things of the

Spirit of God, for they are foolishness to him and he is not able to understand them.

This passage does not teach that unbelievers are intellectually incapable of grasping the meaning of biblical sentences. Many unbelievers can give accurate summaries of the gospel. What they **do not do** is embrace those truths as divine and submit to them. "Does not accept," "folly," and "not able to understand" describe a moral and spiritual refusal, not a lack of mental capacity.

Paul's contrast is between those who reject the Spirit's revelation as foolish and those who receive it as the wisdom of God. Christians have "the mind of Christ" not because the Spirit mystically indwells them as a private tutor, but because the Spirit has given the apostolic message and they have believed it.

How, then, do believers grow in understanding? Not by waiting for special inner flashes, but by doing the hard, reverent work of conservative, grammatical-historical interpretation. We seek the author's meaning in context, paying attention to genre, grammar, history, and the flow of thought. The Spirit's role is to have inspired the text and to use that text to convict and correct us as we study. There is no second stream of private revelation alongside the written Word.

How the Holy Spirit Truly "Dwells" in Believers

Putting all of this together, we can say that the Holy Spirit "dwells" in Christians in four closely related ways, none of which require literal indwelling.

He dwells **representatively** through His Word. Wherever the Scriptures are believed, honored, and obeyed, the Spirit is present in authority. His commandments and promises are the voice that rules that life or congregation.

He dwells **covenantally** by ownership. Believers have been bought with a price. They are a people for Jehovah's own possession. To say the Spirit is in them is to say they are marked out as His, just as the temple in Jerusalem was marked out as His dwelling.

He dwells **ecclesially** in the gathered church. The congregation as a whole is a temple, a house where the Spirit's Word is taught and lived. To damage that unity or corrupt that doctrine is to defile the temple of God.

He dwells **prospectively** by guaranteeing resurrection. The Spirit of the One who raised Jesus from the dead seals believers for the day of redemption. His past act in raising Christ and His present testimony in Scripture guarantee that those in Christ will one day be raised in glory.

All of this is rich, robust, and deeply comforting. It requires no mystical language. It calls us not to search our inner feelings for signs of an invisible Resident, but to anchor our hearts and minds in the written Word the Spirit has breathed out. To walk by the Spirit is to live by that Word. To be filled with the Spirit is to let that Word dwell richly in us. To have the Spirit dwell in us is to be a people ruled, taught, comforted, and corrected by the Scriptures He Himself has given.

CHAPTER 11 The Holy Spirit in the First Century and Today

When modern Christians read Acts and the letters of the apostles, they often feel a sharp contrast between the first-century church and their own experience. In Acts, the Holy Spirit is associated with rushing wind, tongues of fire, healings, prophecies, and direct commands. Today, many congregations gather quietly with Bibles in their hands and no visible miracles. This contrast raises questions. Has the Holy Spirit withdrawn? Should we expect the same signs now? Are we missing something if we do not see what the apostles saw?

The only safe way to answer those questions is to trace carefully what Scripture itself teaches about the Spirit's work in the first century and what it teaches about His work after the completion of the New Testament. When we do that, a clear pattern emerges. The Holy Spirit's activity in the apostolic age was **foundational** and **temporary** in its miraculous forms, aimed at revealing, confirming, and spreading the gospel before the Scriptures were complete. Today the same Holy Spirit works with undiminished power, but He does so **through the finished, Spirit-inspired Word**, not through new revelations, miraculous gifts, or a literal indwelling in believers.

There is one Spirit, one plan of salvation, and one unfolding history. The difference between then and now is not that He has grown weaker, but that He has moved from **building the foundation** to **using that completed foundation** to guide the people of God.

The Holy Spirit in the First Century Church

Pentecost and the Launch of the New Era

The decisive public beginning of the Spirit's first-century work came on the day of Pentecost. The apostles were all together in one place when a sound like a violent rushing wind came from heaven and filled the house. Tongues as of fire appeared and rested on each of them, and they began to speak in other languages as the Spirit gave them utterance.

This event was not a private mystical experience. It was a public, audible, visible sign that the crucified and risen Jesus had been exalted and had poured out the promised Spirit. Peter explained to the crowd that Jesus, now at the right hand of God, had "poured forth this which you both see and hear." The Spirit's work here is tied to **visible signs** and **spoken words**.

Several truths stand out.

First, Pentecost is directly linked to the apostles' mission. Jesus had promised that they would receive power when the Holy Spirit came upon them and that they would be His witnesses in Jerusalem, all Judea and Samaria, and to the remotest part of the earth. The power is given to launch that witness. The Spirit's coming here is not a general experience for all believers in every age; it is a unique empowering of the apostolic band for their foundational work.

Second, the miracle of tongues serves a very specific purpose. Devout Jews from many nations heard the apostles speaking in their own native languages the mighty works of God. The point is not private devotional speech but public proclamation. The Spirit temporarily overcomes language barriers so that the message about Christ can be heard by many nations at once.

Third, Pentecost fulfills Old Testament promises about a new stage in the Spirit's work. Joel had foretold a time when God would pour out His Spirit on all flesh—on sons and daughters, young and old, male and female servants. That prophecy begins to be fulfilled as the Spirit's power, once focused on a few prophets and kings, now spreads widely in the community that confesses Jesus as Messiah.

The key feature in all of this is that the Spirit's work is **historical, observable, and tied to revelation.** He is not giving vague inner impressions; He is establishing the apostolic witness with unmistakable signs.

Miraculous Gifts and Their Purpose

The book of Acts and the letters of Paul show that the first-century congregations experienced a wide range of miraculous gifts. These included prophecy, tongues and their interpretation, healings, miracles, and special acts of knowledge and wisdom. These gifts were not random displays of power. They had clear purposes.

They served to **confirm new revelation**. Hebrews declares that the great salvation "was at the first spoken through the Lord, and it was confirmed to us by those who heard, God also bearing witness with them, both by signs and wonders and by various miracles and by gifts of the Holy Spirit distributed according to his will." The miracles and gifts are God's own testimony that the message the apostles and prophets proclaim is truly from Him.

They helped to **build up congregations** that did not yet have a complete New Testament. A local church with only a few scrolls of the Old Testament and no full collection of apostolic writings needed direct prophetic guidance. Men gifted by the Spirit could speak God's will, warn, instruct, and correct. Tongues and their interpretation allowed the message to be communicated across languages. Gifts of discerning spirits protected against false claims.

They demonstrated that the gospel was for **Jews and Gentiles alike**. When the Spirit fell on Cornelius and those with him, they spoke in other languages and magnified God, just as the apostles had at the beginning. Peter recognized this as the same gift and concluded that God had granted repentance to life even to Gentiles. The Spirit's miraculous work thus broke through racial and religious barriers.

Crucially, these gifts are consistently tied to the **apostolic era**. They cluster around the men who were personally chosen by Christ and those to whom they imparted gifts. They are signs of a new revelation being given and confirmed.

Direct Guidance and Revelation

Alongside the miraculous gifts, the Holy Spirit in the first century gave direct guidance at key junctures. He "said" to the church at Antioch, "Set apart for me Barnabas and Saul for the work to which I have called them." He forbade Paul and his companions to speak the word in certain regions and did not permit them to go into others. Prophets such as Agabus, moved by the Spirit, predicted specific events like famine or imprisonment.

This guidance is always tied to **the progress of the gospel** and the **foundational decisions of the early church.** For example, at the Jerusalem meeting about Gentile believers, the apostles and elders concluded that their decision "seemed good to the Holy Spirit and to us," because it aligned with the prophetic Scriptures and the clear demonstrations God had given.

This kind of direct guidance does not appear as a perpetual promise to every believer in every age. It belongs to the unique situation in which the church is being founded, the canon is not yet complete, and the apostles are still alive to receive and verify such messages.

The Spirit's Presence Without Literal Indwelling

Even in the first century, the language used about the Spirit does not require a literal, spatial indwelling. The Spirit fills, comes upon, rests on, or is poured out. These expressions describe **activity and control**, not location.

When the apostles are filled with the Holy Spirit and speak the word with boldness, it does not mean the Spirit was absent a moment before and then suddenly moved inside them as a new Resident. It means He powerfully takes hold of them for a specific task— preaching in the face of opposition. When elders or deacons are described as full of the Holy Spirit, the meaning is that their lives are dominated by the Spirit's character and Word.

Thus, even in that miracle-rich era, we do not find a doctrine of the Spirit as a permanent inner occupant. We find the same pattern Scripture uses elsewhere: to be "in" the Spirit and to have the Spirit "in" you is to be under His rule, shaped by His revelation, and employed in His service.

From Partial to Complete: The Shift in the Spirit's Work

The New Testament itself explains that the miraculous, piecemeal pattern of the early years was never intended to be permanent. Paul draws a sharp line between the **partial** stage and the **mature** stage.

He writes that "we know in part and we prophesy in part, but when the perfect comes, the partial will be done away with." The "partial" refers to the bits and pieces of revelation delivered through prophecies, tongues, and special knowledge. Congregations were receiving God's message in stages, like children learning step by step.

The "perfect," in contrast, is the complete, mature form of that revelation—the fully delivered faith. Other passages describe this completion. Jude speaks of "the faith which was once for all delivered to the holy ones." Ephesians portrays the church as built on the foundation of the apostles and prophets, with Christ Jesus Himself as the cornerstone. Hebrews states that God spoke in many portions and in many ways in past times, but in these last days He has spoken to us in a Son.

When that foundation is finished, when the apostolic witness has been fully given and written, there is no further need for piecemeal prophetic messages or confirming signs. The building rises on a completed base. Revelation moves from being **given** to being **preserved and applied.**

This is exactly what we see historically. As the apostolic era closes, the emphasis shifts from fresh revelations to guarding the teaching already delivered. Warnings multiply against adding to the gospel, twisting it, or turning to myths and speculative ideas. The Spirit's work is now centered on **protecting, illuminating, and enforcing** the deposit of truth.

In that setting, miraculous gifts fade from the scene because their purpose has been fulfilled. The church no longer needs direct prophetic words to know God's will; it has the Spirit-inspired Scriptures. It no longer needs tongues to authenticate new revelation; it preaches from a completed New Testament.

The Holy Spirit Today: The Same Spirit, a Different Mode

The Holy Spirit in our time is not a different Spirit from the One who acted in the first century. He is the same divine Person, holy and good, who brought the universe into existence, empowered the prophets, anointed Christ, raised Him from the dead, and guided the apostles. What has changed is the **stage of God's plan** and therefore the **way the Spirit carries out His work**.

No Miraculous Gifts, No New Revelation

Today there are no apostles in the New Testament sense. No one alive has personally seen the risen Christ and been commissioned directly by Him to speak with inspired authority. There are no prophets giving new, inerrant words from God. There are no tongues that miraculously cross language barriers as at Pentecost. There are no genuine gifts of healing that allow a person to cure any disease at will.

Claims to such gifts always collapse under biblical scrutiny. Either the supposed miracles are unverifiable, the "prophecies" fail or are vague enough to mean anything, or the teachings that accompany them contradict Scripture. The Spirit does not contradict Himself. He does not inspire the New Testament and then endorse messages that distort it.

The reason miraculous gifts have ceased is not that the Spirit has withdrawn, but that His purpose for those signs has been met. The faith has been fully delivered. The apostolic foundation has been laid. The Scriptures are complete. To continue giving new revelations and confirming signs would be to tear up the foundation and start building again.

The Spirit's Exclusive Instrument: The Written Word

In this age the Holy Spirit works **only through the Spirit-inspired Scriptures**. He does not bypass the written Word with private whisperings, inner voices, or mystical impressions. He speaks when the Bible speaks.

When believers open Scripture with reverent faith, the Spirit is active. He does not reveal new meanings hidden from others. He presses the true meaning of the text on the conscience. He uses the law to expose sin, the narratives to show God's ways, the prophecies to display His faithfulness, the Gospels to present Christ, and the letters to instruct in doctrine and conduct.

The process is not magical. Understanding comes through study: attention to context, grammar, historical background, and the flow of thought. The Spirit's role is to have given a perfectly sufficient text and to use that text to challenge, comfort, and change those who submit to it.

Faith comes from hearing the Word of Christ. Holiness comes from obeying the Word. Comfort comes from believing the promises of the Word. In every case, the Spirit is at work because the Word is His own voice.

No Literal Indwelling of the Holy Spirit

In keeping with the previous chapter, it must be stated plainly again: **there is no literal indwelling of the Holy Spirit in Christians today.** The Spirit does not move into the physical body of the believer as an extra Person living inside.

All the passages that speak of the Spirit "dwelling in" believers, or being "in" them, or being "sent into their hearts," can be and must be understood in light of biblical usage. The same language is used of the Word dwelling in us, faith dwelling in us, love dwelling in us, and Christ dwelling in our hearts. These are relational and covenant expressions.

To say that the Spirit dwells in believers is to say that they live under His rule, shaped by His revelation, marked out as His possession, and secured by His promise of resurrection. The Spirit's presence and influence come through His Word. There is no second stream of personal influence inside the believer apart from that Word.

No Divine Testing Through Trials

It is also important to reject a common misunderstanding about the Spirit's role in difficulties. Many teach that God sends trials in order to test and refine His people, as if He designs painful circumstances for the purpose of spiritual improvement. This concept contradicts the clear statements of Scripture.

James insists that when a person is under trial, he must not say, "I am being tried by God," for God is not tried by evil and He Himself does not try anyone. Evil circumstances, temptations to sin, and crushing hardships do not originate from Jehovah. They arise from a fallen world, human imperfection, and the malice of Satan and demons. Jehovah permits these realities because He has granted genuine freedom, but He does not author them.

The Holy Spirit therefore does not "test" believers by orchestrating tragedies. His work in suffering is to **comfort and strengthen through the Word**, not to design calamity. When a believer faces hardship, the Spirit speaks through Scripture to assure him of God's love, to remind him of Christ's example, and to call him to faithfulness. The trial itself is not the Spirit's tool; the Word is.

The Spirit's Present Work in Believers and the Church

Sanctification by the Spirit and the Truth

The Spirit's ongoing work in Christians is especially seen in sanctification. God chose believers for salvation "through sanctification by the Spirit and faith in the truth." Sanctification happens as the Spirit uses the truth to renew the mind and reshape conduct.

The Bible calls believers to put off the old person and put on the new, to be transformed by the renewing of their minds, and to walk in a manner worthy of the calling they have received. None of this is automatic. It requires deliberate obedience to commands, imitation of Christ, and constant repentance when we fall short.

As Christians practice these things in dependence on the Word, the Spirit is at work. The fruit of the Spirit—love, joy, peace, patience, kindness, goodness, faithfulness, gentleness, self-control—emerges in their lives because they are living according to the patterns He has revealed. He does not inject these qualities into the heart apart from

Scripture; He produces them through the believer's sustained response to Scripture.

Guidance by the Spirit Through the Word

The Spirit also guides believers. But His guidance is not a private voice telling someone which job to take, which house to buy, or which route to drive. His guidance is the wisdom of Scripture applied to real decisions.

The Word lays down clear commands that must never be violated. It also gives principles that must be weighed: priorities in life, warnings about greed, the value of honest work, the importance of caring for family, the call to seek first God's kingdom. When a believer studies these things, prays for wisdom, receives counsel from mature brothers, and then makes a decision in line with biblical principles, he is being led by the Spirit.

To be "led by the Spirit" is to live under the direction of the Spirit's teaching instead of being driven by the desires of the flesh. This is how Paul uses the phrase in Romans 8. Those who are led by the Spirit are the sons of God because they obey the Spirit's revealed will rather than the impulses of sin.

Assurance by the Spirit's Testimony in the Word

The Spirit also gives assurance. Romans 8:16 says that "the Spirit himself testifies with our spirit that we are children of God." This is often misunderstood as an inner whisper. In reality, the Spirit testifies in Scripture, describing who the children of God are: those who have believed the gospel, repented, been baptized into Christ, and who now walk according to the Spirit's teaching instead of according to the flesh.

Our own spirit "testifies with" His when we compare our faith and life to that description and see that, though imperfect, we truly belong to that group. The Spirit's witness in the Word and our conscience's witness about our actual condition line up, and assurance grows.

If someone claims assurance while ignoring Scripture, living in unrepentant sin, or embracing false doctrine, then his inner confidence does not match the Spirit's testimony. In that case, the Spirit does not testify that such a person is a child of God. Assurance is anchored in the objective Word, not in fluctuating feelings.

Help in Prayer in Harmony with the Word

Romans 8:26–27 speaks of the Spirit helping believers in their weakness, interceding with groanings too deep for words. This is not a description of private prayer languages or unconscious utterances. It is a description of the Spirit's alignment of the believer's prayers with the will of God.

We often do not know how to pray as we should, especially in times of intense suffering or confusion. Yet as we cling to the truths of Scripture, the Spirit shapes our desires and requests. Even when we can barely form sentences and can only groan before God, He who searches hearts knows what the mind of the Spirit is, because the Spirit always intercedes according to God's will.

The Spirit's help here is not in giving us new content outside the Bible, but in ensuring that our prayers—however feeble—are framed and interpreted in light of the revealed purposes of God.

Learning From the First Century, Living in This One

The first-century church stands before us as a vivid demonstration of what the Holy Spirit can do. He empowered simple men to preach boldly, confirmed their message with undeniable signs, carried the gospel across cultural barriers, and produced congregations marked by love, courage, and endurance.

We are not called to **reproduce** every feature of that era. We are not to seek new apostles, new revelations, or new miracles. We are called to **receive** the apostolic message they left and to be as faithful to that message in our age as they were in theirs.

The same Holy Spirit who spoke through them has preserved their writings for us. He now calls us to open those writings, understand them with sound, conservative methods, reject the speculations of modern criticism, and obey what we find there.

When we do that, we are as truly "Spirit-filled" as any believer has ever been—not because we feel a certain way, but because our hearts and minds are saturated with the Word He breathed out. The difference between the first century and today is not in the Spirit's power but in the stage of His plan. They saw the foundation laid; we build on that completed foundation. They heard the voice of the Spirit through living apostles; we hear the same voice through the completed Scriptures.

In every age, those who truly honor the Holy Spirit are not those who chase experiences, but those who bow before His Word.

CHAPTER 12 Understanding the Role and Work of the Holy Spirit

The earlier chapters of this book have shown that the Holy Spirit is a divine Person, that He acted in unique ways in the first century to reveal and confirm the gospel, and that He now works through the completed, Spirit-inspired Scriptures. This chapter draws those lines together in several practical areas where Christians often feel confused or fearful: blasphemy against the Spirit, the fruit of the Spirit, Christian living, prayer, assurance, and guidance.

In all of these themes, one truth must remain clear: **the Holy Spirit does not literally indwell believers as a mystical inner Guest.** He works in and among Christians **through the Word He has inspired**.

He does not whisper fresh messages, nor does He design painful events to "test" believers. Difficulties arise from human imperfection, Satan, demons, and a wicked world. The Spirit's task is to confront, comfort, and change us by means of Scripture, not to send calamities.

With that in mind, we can now look carefully at how the Bible itself describes His role and work.

Blasphemy Against the Holy Spirit

The Historical Setting in Matthew 12

Blasphemy against the Holy Spirit is one of the most sobering subjects in the New Testament. Many tender-hearted believers are troubled by Jesus' warning that this sin "will not be forgiven, either in this age or in the age to come." Some fear that a stray thought or careless comment has placed them beyond mercy. Scripture provides strong reasons to calm such fear.

The key passage is Matthew 12. Jesus had been under relentless attack from the Pharisees. They watched Him with hostile eyes, not to learn, but to find grounds to accuse Him. When His disciples plucked heads of grain on the Sabbath, they pounced. When He healed a man with a withered hand, they began plotting His death. Their hearts were not neutral; they were already set against Him.

Then they brought to Jesus a man who was demon-possessed, blind, and mute. Jesus healed him so that he spoke and saw. The crowds, recognizing that such power belonged to God, began to ask whether this might be the Son of David. They were at least open to the conclusion that Jesus was the promised Messiah.

The Pharisees could not deny the miracle; the man stood before them changed. Yet instead of submitting to what the Spirit of God had clearly done, they said, "This man does not cast out demons except by Beelzebub the ruler of the demons." They deliberately attributed an undeniable work of the Spirit to Satan.

Jesus showed the absurdity of their charge. If Satan is casting out Satan, his kingdom is divided against itself. But if Jesus casts out demons by the Spirit of God, then the kingdom of God has come upon them. He then issued His solemn warning about blasphemy against the Spirit.

Why Their Sin Was Uniquely Serious

What made their situation so serious was not a momentary doubt or a hasty word. It was a **settled, stubborn rejection of overwhelming light**. These men were not ignorant pagans. They knew the Scriptures. They had seen and heard Christ's works. They watched a demon cast out in a way that their own traditions recognized as a work of God. In full knowledge, they chose to label the Spirit's activity as satanic.

In other words, they stood at the highest level of revelation short of the final events of the cross and resurrection, and they responded with willful slander. Their mouths were expressing what their hearts had already become: fully hardened, hostile to the truth, devoted to their own position and power even if it meant calling the Holy Spirit's work the work of demons.

Jesus' warning did not mean they had already crossed a hidden line, but that they were dangerously close. If they continued down that path, constantly rejecting the Spirit's testimony and calling His clearest works evil, they would pass into a state in which repentance would never occur and forgiveness would never be received.

What Blasphemy Against the Spirit Is

Blasphemy against the Holy Spirit, then, is **not** a careless phrase, an intrusive thought, or a single angry outburst. It is **a settled, deliberate, lifelong rejection and slandering of the Spirit's witness to Christ**, in full knowledge of what one is doing.

In the unique setting of Jesus' earthly ministry, that meant looking directly at miracles done by the Spirit, hearing teaching that perfectly fulfilled the Scriptures, and then calling that work satanic. In the broader New Testament pattern, it parallels the person who has been surrounded by clear apostolic teaching, has tasted the blessings of Christian fellowship, has seen the power of the gospel at work, and yet finally turns away in open, hostile repudiation, calling the truth a lie and the Spirit's testimony deceitful.

Passages such as Hebrews 6 and Hebrews 10 describe such people: not those who stumble and weep over their sins, but those who knowingly trample the Son of God underfoot and insult the Spirit of grace. For such a person, there is no further sacrifice for sins, not because God has grown unwilling to forgive, but because the sinner has hardened himself past any desire for repentance.

Why Anxious Believers Have Not Committed It

This biblical picture immediately exposes a common fear as unfounded. A person who has actually committed blasphemy against the Holy Spirit **would have no concern that he had done so**. His heart would be hardened, his conscience seared. He would not be asking whether he had sinned too greatly; he would be openly despising the very idea of forgiveness.

If someone is grieved, afraid of offending God, troubled over sin, and eager to seek mercy in Christ, that very concern is evidence that the Spirit is still using Scripture to convict. Such a person has not committed the unforgivable sin. He needs to be pointed to the promises that Christ receives all who come to Him in obedient faith.

The right response to Jesus' warning is not morbid self-torment, but **humble reverence**. We must never treat lightly the Spirit's testimony in Scripture. We must never play with the idea of calling truth "false" or the gospel "evil." Instead we bow before the Word, repent where it exposes us, and cling to the Savior it presents.

Persistent Rejection and Final Hardening

The principle behind this sin remains vital today. The Holy Spirit still bears witness to Christ—not by fresh miracles, but by the written Word. When that Word is preached, read, taught, and obeyed, the Spirit speaks. When it is persistently resisted, the heart hardens.

The danger is not that a believer may accidentally cross a line without realizing it, but that a hearer may repeatedly shrug off the Spirit's warnings until he cares nothing for them. The same sun that melts wax hardens clay. The same gospel that softens one heart drives another deeper into defiance.

Therefore, understanding blasphemy against the Spirit should move us to serious listening. Each time Scripture is opened we are hearing the Spirit's own voice. To respond with humble faith is to honor Him. To respond with growing indifference or hostility is to walk a path that, if never left, ends in irreversible hardness.

Edward D. Andrews

The Fruit of the Spirit and the Spirit-Governed Life

The Spirit's Fruit as Christlike Character

If blasphemy against the Spirit shows the worst form of resistance to His work, the "fruit of the Spirit" shows the positive beauty of a life governed by His Word. Paul describes that fruit in Galatians:

But the fruit of the Spirit is love, joy, peace, patience, kindness, goodness, faithfulness, gentleness, self-control; against such things there is no law.

These qualities are not mystical sensations; they are **observable character traits** that reflect the likeness of Christ. They stand in stark contrast to the works of the flesh that Paul lists in the same passage: immorality, idolatry, outbursts of anger, divisions, drunkenness, and similar behaviors.

To say that these virtues are the Spirit's fruit is to say that they arise when a person's heart and conduct are brought under the Spirit's teaching. The Spirit has given the Scriptures that reveal Jehovah's character and Christ's example. As believers submit to that revelation, their lives gradually take on the same traits.

How the Spirit Produces Fruit Through the Word

The Spirit does not produce fruit by bypassing our minds and choices. He produces it by working through **truth understood, believed, and applied.**

Paul says, "Do not be conformed to this world, but be transformed by the renewing of your mind." That renewal comes as the Word of God is taken in, meditated on, and obeyed. The Spirit who inspired that Word uses it to re-train our thinking. Old patterns of selfishness, bitterness, and impurity are challenged and replaced by new patterns of love, gratitude, and purity.

In another place Paul tells believers to "put off the old man" and "put on the new man," which is created according to God in righteousness and holiness of the truth. The "old man" is our former way of life, shaped by sin. The "new man" is the new pattern of life that matches what God has revealed. The Holy Spirit's role is to expose the old through the Word and to set before us the new, then to press our conscience until we actually make different choices.

This means that cultivating the fruit of the Spirit is **never passive**. It is not waiting for a feeling, but actively bringing our desires and decisions under the authority of Scripture. For example, when we are tempted to respond harshly, we recall that the Spirit commands gentleness. When resentment rises, we remember that love "keeps no account of the injury." When anxiety swells, we remember that the Spirit directs us to cast our cares on Jehovah and to think on what is true and praiseworthy. Each act of obedience plants and waters the fruit He is producing.

Putting off the Old Person and Putting on the New

Living by the Spirit, therefore, involves deliberate replacement. The thief must no longer steal but must work, so that he may have something to share. The liar must lay aside falsehood and speak the truth. The one given to corrupt speech must replace it with words that build up.

These changes are not achieved by sheer willpower apart from the Spirit, nor are they achieved by waiting for a mystical transformation apart from effort. They are achieved as the Spirit's Word lays claim to each area of life and the believer responds with practical obedience. In that process the Spirit is truly at work, yet always through the Scriptures He has given.

The Holy Spirit and Christian Living

Walking by the Spirit

When Paul urges believers to "walk by the Spirit," he is not calling them to chase impressions. He is calling them to **live in step with the Spirit's teaching**. The alternative is walking according to the flesh, that is, according to sinful desires and the world's patterns.

To walk by the Spirit is to let His Word set the direction for every relationship, responsibility, and habit. It means submitting our attitudes toward work, family, money, speech, leisure, and service to the commands and principles of Scripture. When a congregation as a whole is governed by the Word in this way, it can truly be said that the Spirit is active in that church.

Strength to Put Sin to Death

Romans 8 speaks of believers putting to death the deeds of the body "by the Spirit." This does not mean the Spirit performs the obedience for us. It means that the Spirit has given the truth about sin's seriousness, has revealed the way of escape in Christ, and has promised strength to those who rely on God. As we use that truth in our fight against temptation, the Spirit's power is at work.

The believer who fills his mind with Scripture, prays for help, and then refuses to yield to sin is not acting in mere human strength. He is acting in the strength supplied by the Spirit through the Word. That is genuine spiritual warfare, grounded not in spectacle, but in day-to-day obedience.

The Role of the Holy Spirit in Prayer

The Spirit's Help in Our Weakness

Prayer is another area where Christians often inject mystical ideas about the Spirit's work. Romans 8:26–27 provides a sober, comforting perspective:

In the same way the Spirit also helps our weakness; for we do not know how to pray as we should, but the Spirit himself intercedes for us with groanings too deep for words; and he who searches the hearts knows what the mind of the Spirit is, because he intercedes for the holy ones according to the will of God.

We are weak. We often lack wisdom. In hard circumstances we may not know what specifically to ask. Yet even then, as we come to God in dependence, anchoring our thoughts in Scripture, the Spirit is at work. He shapes our desires through the Word so that, even when our words falter, our heart's direction lines up with the will of God.

The "groanings too deep for words" are not a secret prayer language given to believers. They describe the depth of our distress and the Spirit's perfect understanding of that distress. He translates our inarticulate cries into petitions that fit the Father's wise plan.

Praying in the Spirit

Ephesians calls believers to pray "in the Spirit." This does not mean entering a special trancelike state. It means praying **in harmony with the Spirit's revelation.** To pray in the Spirit is to let the themes, promises, and priorities of Scripture shape our requests.

For example, the Spirit has revealed that we should pray for the spread of the gospel, for the strengthening of believers, for wisdom to live uprightly, for boldness in witness, and for the coming of Christ's Kingdom. When those concerns dominate our prayers, we are praying in the Spirit.

We dishonor the Spirit when we ignore Scripture and treat prayer as a way to chase our own desires. We honor Him when we pray from a mind saturated with the Word, asking that God would accomplish what the Spirit has already declared important.

Assurance and Guidance From the Holy Spirit

The Spirit's Testimony with Our Spirit

Romans 8:16 says, "The Spirit himself testifies with our spirit that we are children of God." This is often misunderstood as a feeling that suddenly descends, telling a person he is saved. Scripture itself gives a clearer explanation.

The Spirit testifies in the **objective promises and descriptions of Scripture.** He tells us who the children of God are: those who have believed the gospel, repented, been baptized into Christ, and who now walk according to the Spirit rather than according to the flesh. Our own spirit, that is, our conscience and self-knowledge, testifies about whether that description fits us.

When the Spirit's description in the Word and our honest self-examination agree, assurance grows. If we see that we have obeyed the gospel and that, despite our many failings, we are fighting sin and seeking to live under the Word, then we have strong reason to conclude that we are indeed children of God.

If, on the other hand, someone lives in open rebellion, cares nothing for Scripture, and yet claims inner assurance of salvation, his personal feeling contradicts the Spirit's testimony. In such a case, the "witness" he relies on is not the Holy Spirit.

Guidance Through the Word, Not Private Voices

The Holy Spirit also guides believers. But He guides them primarily and sufficiently **through Scripture**. Proverbs calls us to trust in Jehovah with all our heart, not lean on our own understanding, acknowledge Him in all our ways, and He will make our paths straight. That straightening happens as we submit our decisions to the light of the Word.

When facing choices about work, relationships, or service, we ask: Does this path violate any command? Does it pull me away from the congregation? Does it foster greed, impurity, or pride? Does it hinder my responsibilities to family? What priorities has the Spirit set in Scripture? We then choose the option that best aligns with those principles, praying for wisdom.

There is no need, and no biblical warrant, to wait for a mysterious "leading" apart from the Word. To look for such voices is to open the door to self-deception. The Spirit's guidance is clear, stable, and public—written for all to see.

The Spirit's Role and Our Responsibility

Understanding the role and work of the Holy Spirit does not diminish His importance; it restores Him to His rightful place. He is not a vague feeling or a private whisper. He is the divine Author of Scripture, the One who speaks whenever the Bible is faithfully proclaimed, the One who convicts the world, gives new life through the gospel, produces fruit in obedient believers, strengthens them in weakness, and assures them of their adoption.

At the same time, this understanding guards us from passivity. Because the Spirit works through the Word, Christians must be people of the Word. We cannot expect growth if we neglect Scripture. We cannot expect guidance if we ignore the commands and principles already revealed. We cannot claim the Spirit's comfort while despising His message.

Blasphemy against the Spirit is hardened rejection of His testimony; honoring the Spirit is humble submission to that testimony. Every time we open the Bible with a willing heart, we are placing ourselves under His gracious work. Every step of obedience taken in response to Scripture is a step "by the Spirit."

The more clearly we grasp this, the more confidently we can live. We do not have to chase experiences or wonder whether the Spirit has abandoned us because we lack miracles. We have His completed Word in our hands. We have His call to repent, believe, obey, and hope. As we do so, He is active—quietly, powerfully, and faithfully— until the day when Christ returns and the Spirit's work in the church reaches its final, glorious goal.

CHAPTER 13 From Spoken Word to Sacred Text: The Human Hands Behind an Inerrant New Testament

When a Christian opens the New Testament today, it is easy to imagine each book quietly written by a solitary apostle seated at a desk. The real picture is far more vivid. Letters were dictated aloud in busy rooms. Skilled secretaries listened and wrote. Trusted carriers walked roads and sailed seas with single handwritten copies. Congregations gathered as those letters were read aloud again and again. Behind every word stood the Holy Spirit as divine Author, using very human means to give a fully inerrant written Word that would outlive empires.

This chapter explains how that happened. We will trace how New Testament books were first composed, how early Christian scribes and carriers served the apostolic authors, and how this entire process fits with verbal, plenary inspiration and inerrancy. We will also face a crucial question: if the Holy Spirit inspired fallible men, and those men used fallible scribes, how can we still speak of an inerrant New Testament?

Writing in the World of the New Testament

Modern writers often crave silence and isolation. They withdraw to offices or studies, close the door, and try to shut out every distraction. The world of the apostles was the opposite. Ancient people lived and worked in shared spaces. Shops were open to the street. Houses were crowded. Reading and writing were often done in the midst of conversation and movement.

The apostle Paul almost certainly did not sit alone in a private "study." When he composed a letter, he would usually be in a house full of fellow workers, hosts, and visitors. Others could hear him dictate. Questions might be asked. Names might be suggested to greet. Instead of hindering him, this setting fit the social habits of the time. People were used to thinking, speaking, and even composing with others around them.

In that environment, writing was not usually done by the main speaker himself. Professional or semi-professional scribes were common in the Greco-Roman world. Government officials used scribes. Wealthy households used scribes. Businesses used scribes. And the apostles, especially Paul, used scribes as well.

Amanuenses and Secretaries

The technical term for such a helper is *amanuensis*—a secretary who writes for another. In Romans 16:22 we hear the voice of one such man: "I Tertius, the one who write the letter, greet you in the Lord." Paul is the inspired author of Romans; Tertius is the trained hand who wrote as Paul spoke.

Ancient secretaries could serve at different levels. Some simply took dictation, word by word. Some were capable of shorthand and would later write out a fair copy. In other settings, a wealthy patron might give a secretary a general idea and allow him to compose an ordinary letter. That last model, however, does not fit the New Testament.

For several reasons we must insist that New Testament amanuenses did not create the content of the books. The apostolic writers constantly claim personal responsibility for what is written. Paul speaks of "the things that I am writing to you" and insists that "the things which I write to you are the Lord's commandment" (1 Corinthians 14:37). He reminds the Thessalonians, "I, Paul, write this greeting with my own hand, which is a distinguishing mark in every letter; this is the way I write" (2 Thessalonians 3:17). A secretary might hold the pen for most of the document, but the thoughts, arguments, and words are Paul's.

There is also a simple practical reason. Early Christian congregations knew the apostles personally. Many heard them preach and saw their character over years. The idea that an unnamed secretary secretly composed major theological letters while the apostle merely attached his name does not fit with the transparent honesty demanded in those same letters. The Holy Spirit inspired chosen men—Matthew, Mark, Luke, John, Paul, Peter, James, Jude—not anonymous literary assistants.

How, then, did dictation actually work? Ancient sources show that skilled scribes could write at normal speaking speed. Less experienced scribes required the speaker to slow down, and sometimes even to speak syllable by syllable. Professional scribes, however, were capable of following continuous speech. Complaints by ancient teachers about being "rushed" by a fast secretary show that the difficulty sometimes lay in keeping up with the writer, not the other way around.

We should picture Paul pacing or sitting, speaking sentence after sentence, perhaps pausing to shape a difficult phrase, while a trained amanuensis like Tertius steadily wrote on papyrus sheets with a reed pen. When the dictation session was finished, Paul would review what had been written, make any corrections, and then approve the final text.

The Divine Author Behind Human Authors

All of this was ordinary human activity. Yet something extraordinary was happening at the same time. The Holy Spirit was actively moving certain men so that what they spoke—and therefore what their scribes wrote—was exactly the Word of God.

Paul states it simply: "All Scripture is inspired by God and profitable for teaching, for reproof, for correction, for training in righteousness, so that the man of God may be fully competent, equipped for every good work" (2 Timothy 3:16–17). The key expression "inspired by God" literally means "God-breathed." Scripture is not merely a record of religious experiences; it is the direct out-breathing of God in written form.

Peter explains the same truth from another angle: "no prophecy was ever produced by the will of man, but men carried along by the

Holy Spirit spoke from God" (2 Peter 1:21). The human writers did not decide on their own to produce God's Word. They were "carried along" by the Holy Spirit. The verb is used elsewhere for a ship driven along by the wind. The sailors are real, active, and responsible, but the driving force is outside them.

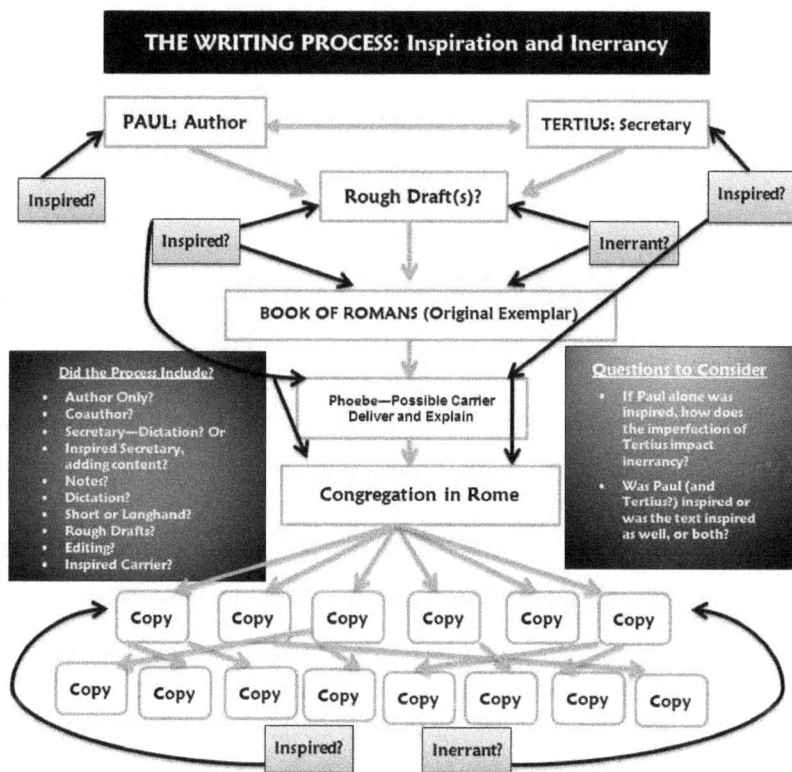

THE WRITING PROCESS: Inspiration and Inerrancy

When we bring these passages together, several truths stand out.

First, inspiration concerns the writings themselves. "All Scripture is inspired by God." The product—the written text—is God-breathed. That is why Jesus can quote a line from the Old Testament and say, "Have you not read what was spoken to you by God?" The written text of Scripture is God speaking.

Second, inspiration is verbal and plenary. Verbal means that inspiration reaches down to the very words, not just to vague ideas. Plenary means that all of Scripture is inspired, not merely selected parts. The Holy Spirit did not simply plant general thoughts while leaving the wording to chance. He used each writer's vocabulary, style, and personality, but He superintended the process so that the words chosen expressed exactly what He intended to say.

Third, inspiration belongs to the original writings, the autographs produced under the Spirit's direct superintendence. Copies and translations are the Word of God to the extent that they faithfully reproduce those originals. When Paul dictated Romans, the first completed copy—the text he approved and sent—is the inspired, inerrant autograph.

Fourth, the Holy Spirit's role in inspiration does not cancel the humanity of the authors. Their background, experiences, and writing habits remain. Luke researches and arranges material carefully. John writes with a distinctive style. Paul's argumentation reflects his training. Yet the Spirit guards everything so that what they write is fully truthful, without error in anything it affirms.

The amanuensis fits into this picture as a tool, not as an inspired co-author. The Spirit did not bypass the author and secretly move the hand of the scribe. He moved the chosen writer. The scribe's job was to write what the inspired man spoke and to copy that text accurately.

Scribes, Carriers, and the Circulation of the Texts

Once the apostolic author was satisfied with the dictated text, that first copy had to travel. Trusted coworkers served as carriers. Phoebe likely carried the letter to the Romans (Romans 16:1–2). Tychicus carried letters to the Ephesians, the Colossians, and to

Philemon. These men and women were not anonymous delivery people. They were "beloved brothers" and "faithful ministers," often able to explain the circumstances behind the letter and answer questions.

When a carrier arrived, the congregation would gather and the letter would be read aloud from beginning to end. Most believers did not own personal copies. Many could not read. Public reading made the Word accessible to the entire congregation. Paul insisted that this reading take place: "I put you under oath before the Lord to have this letter read to all the brothers" (1 Thessalonians 5:27).

Letters were not meant to remain with a single congregation. Paul instructs the Colossians, "When this letter has been read among you, have it also read in the church of the Laodiceans; and see that you also read the letter from Laodicea" (Colossians 4:16). From the beginning, apostolic writings were shared, copied, and circulated.

Who did the copying? In many congregations a wealthy believer might employ a professional scribe. In other places a Christian who had some training would do the work. Writing a substantial book like Romans or Luke required knowledge of papyrus preparation, ink mixtures, layout, and careful penmanship. The scribe had to rule lines, prick margins, and maintain consistent columns. He might copy by looking back and forth between exemplar and new sheet (eye-to-hand copying), or he might write as someone read aloud from the exemplar (dictation copying).

Very early, Christians favored the codex (book-form) rather than the scroll. Codices were easier to handle, allowed writing on both sides of the page, and could hold more text. Christians also developed distinctive conventions such as *nomina sacra*—abbreviations with a line over them for sacred names like God, Lord, Jesus, Christ, and Spirit. These features show that Christian scribes were not careless.

They were intentionally producing books they believed to be Holy Scripture.

Over time, individual letters began to be collected. A congregation that possessed several letters from Paul might have them copied together into a single codex. A church that had a Gospel might seek copies of other Gospels. By the end of the first century and into the second, collections of apostolic writings were already circulating.

From Autographs to Copies: Does Human Imperfection Destroy Inerrancy?

At this point a thoughtful believer might ask: if only the autographs were inspired, and if copyists were ordinary, fallible people, do copying mistakes overturn inerrancy or undermine confidence in Scripture?

The answer is no, for several reasons.

First, the inspired authors themselves normally checked what their scribes wrote before the first copy left their hands. A scribe like Tertius could make slips of the pen while writing Romans. But Paul was present. He could read the document, correct any errors, and only then allow it to be sent. Inspiration guarantees that the final form of that original letter accurately expressed what the Holy Spirit intended. The scribe's temporary slips did not become part of Scripture.

Second, later copying mistakes do not change what was originally written. Inerrancy is a statement about what God did when He breathed out His Word through the prophets and apostles, not a claim that every later copyist would be miraculously preserved from minor error. Jehovah chose to give perfect autographs and then to preserve their wording through a multitude of ordinary copies. Human weaknesses in copying do not erase the reality of what was first written.

Third, the very abundance and early spread of manuscripts allows us to recover the original wording with extremely high accuracy. Different congregations in different regions copied the same writings. When copies are compared, places where scribes accidentally left out a word, repeated a line, or made a small change can be detected. Because the Holy Spirit led the church to value and preserve these texts, we now possess many hundreds of Greek manuscripts and ancient translations. Careful comparison of these witnesses shows that the New Testament text is stable and that the remaining variations are small and do not alter any doctrine. The Hebrew Old Testament is similarly well preserved.

Fourth, inspiration and inerrancy are not fragile. They do not depend on every copy being flawless. Rather, they rest on the fact that God has given His Word in written form and has so preserved it that the church today can know with confidence what He originally caused to be written. When a modern translation is based on sound textual work and faithfully reflects that original wording, it is truly the Word of God for His people.

Were Scribes and Carriers Inspired?

Another question sometimes raised is whether secretaries like Tertius or carriers like Phoebe were inspired in the same sense as Paul. The answer must be no.

Only those men whom God chose as authors of Scripture were moved by the Holy Spirit so that the result of their writing is the very Word of God. The Spirit did not grant Tertius a new revelation or authority equal to Paul. He did not breathe out Scripture through Phoebe. They served in noble and essential roles, but their function was instrumental, not revelatory.

Several observations confirm this.

Paul distinguishes between his own inspired writing and the help of others. He may mention the one who "writes the letter," but he signs with his own hand as the mark of authenticity. Old Testament patterns are similar. Jeremiah dictates to Baruch, who writes "all the words of Jehovah that he had spoken to him" on a scroll (Jeremiah 36:4). Baruch's skill matters, but the prophetic authority belongs to Jeremiah.

If scribes were inspired in the same sense as authors, Paul would not need to review their work. There would be no need to sign letters as genuine. There would be no concern about forged letters falsely claiming to be from Paul. Yet Paul warns the Thessalonians about such forgeries and points to his own handwriting as proof (2 Thessalonians 2:2; 3:17). This shows that inspiration attaches to the apostolic author, not automatically to anyone who holds a pen.

Recognizing this does not diminish the dignity of the scribes. They were fellow workers who used their training to serve the church. Their careful work was one of the means by which the Holy Spirit gave and preserved Scripture. But the authority of the message comes from Jehovah, through His chosen authors, not from the professional skills of those who copied or carried the text.

The Holy Spirit and the Reading Church

The same Holy Spirit who breathed out the New Testament through apostles and prophets continues to work today through the written Word. He does not repeat the act of inspiration. He is not adding new books or giving new authoritative revelations to modern writers. Instead, He bears witness to the Scriptures He has already given and opens minds to understand and embrace their message.

When a congregation listens as Scripture is read, the Holy Spirit is active. When believers study carefully, seeking the original meaning of each text through the conservative grammatical-historical method, the Spirit is active. When an unbeliever hears the gospel from Romans or John and is convicted of sin and led to faith in Christ, the Spirit is active—through the Word He inspired and preserved.

This is why the book-writing process of the New Testament matters so deeply for churchgoers. It shows that our faith does not rest on vague spiritual impressions or secret inner messages. It rests on a concrete, historical work of God. At a definite time, in real cities, real men moved by the Holy Spirit spoke and wrote. Skilled secretaries and faithful carriers served them. Early Christian scribes copied and shared those writings. Through that chain of events Jehovah has given His people a stable, written, fully trustworthy Bible.

When we hold the New Testament in our hands, we are not dealing with a fragile human product, nor with a mystical document that fell from heaven apart from history. We are reading the Spirit-breathed Word of God, produced through the real labors of authors and scribes, preserved across centuries, and still powerful to teach, reprove, correct, and train in righteousness so that every man and woman of God may be fully competent, equipped for every good work.

CHAPTER 14 Introduction to the Historical Grammatical Method of Biblical Interpretation

Why the Historical-Grammatical Method Matters

Every chapter of this book assumes one simple conviction: the same Holy Spirit who moved the prophets and apostles to write Scripture now directs Christians through that completed, written Word. If that is so, then how we interpret the Bible is not a minor academic preference. It is the difference between submitting to what

God has said and reshaping His message according to our own feelings, traditions, or philosophies.

The Historical-Grammatical Method is simply a disciplined way of asking one basic question of every passage: *What did the human author, moved by the Holy Spirit, intend to say to his original audience, in the words he actually used, in the world in which they actually lived?* When we answer that question accurately, we are then ready to ask a second: *How does that same Spirit-given meaning apply to us today?*

This method assumes that Scripture is clear, coherent, and truthful. It rejects the idea that the "real" meaning of a passage lies buried beneath the text, to be discovered only by a special elite or by speculative theories. The meaning is in the text itself, in its vocabulary, grammar, historical setting, and literary form. The Spirit has not hidden His message behind riddles or codes; He has spoken in ordinary human language that can be carefully studied and rightly understood.

The Bible as Spirit-Breathed and Sufficient

The Historical-Grammatical Method rests on what Scripture claims about itself. Paul writes, "All Scripture is inspired by God and profitable for teaching, for reproof, for correction, for training in righteousness, so that the man of God may be fully competent, equipped for every good work." The phrase "inspired by God" means "God-breathed." Scripture does not become the Word of God when it speaks to us; it *is* the Word of God because God breathed it out through the human writers.

Peter says the same from another angle: "No prophecy of Scripture comes from someone's own interpretation. For no prophecy was ever produced by the will of man, but men spoke from God as they were carried along by the Holy Spirit." The prophets did not push their own ideas upward toward Heaven. The Holy Spirit carried them along, guiding their thoughts and words so that what they wrote can rightly be called the speech of God Himself.

If Scripture is God-breathed and completely sufficient to equip the believer "for every good work," then the task of interpretation is not to complete or correct the Bible but to understand and obey what God has already given. The Historical-Grammatical Method honors this by insisting that our first duty is to hear the text on its own terms instead of forcing it to answer questions it never asked or to fit systems it never taught.

What the Historical-Grammatical Method Seeks to Do

At its core this method asks four interconnected questions.

First, what was happening in history when this passage was written? Second, how do the actual words and grammar function in their sentences and paragraphs? Third, what kind of literature are we reading—law, narrative, poetry, proverb, prophecy, letter, or apocalyptic vision? Fourth, how does this passage fit within the flow of the book and of the whole canon of Scripture?

None of this requires mystical experiences or hidden knowledge. It requires reverent thinking, careful reading, and an honest willingness to let the text say what it says, even when that cuts across our traditions or preferences. The Holy Spirit does not whisper new meanings behind the words; He presses the original meaning of the words upon our minds and consciences as we read and study.

Grasping the Historical Setting

The World of the Author and the Audience

The Holy Spirit did not give Scripture in a vacuum. Every book was written at a particular time, in a particular place, to people who faced specific situations. The Psalms arise from the worship and struggles of Israel. The prophets thundered in days of idolatry, political threat, and spiritual compromise. The Gospels were written in the shadow of Rome's power and Israel's expectations. The letters address real congregations with real sins, fears, and questions.

When Paul writes to Romans, he addresses believers living in the capital of the empire, where Jewish and Gentile Christians were learning to live together as one people in Christ. When he says the gospel is "the power of God for salvation to everyone who believes, to the Jew first and also to the Greek," that statement sits inside sharp tensions about the law of Moses, circumcision, and the place of Israel. Without that historical setting we might sentimentalize the verse and miss its force: in a divided world, God's one way of salvation cuts across every boundary and unites all who believe.

Examples From Old and New Testament

When Jehovah gives the Ten Commandments at Sinai, He speaks to a recently delivered people who had known slavery and paganism. "You shall have no other gods before me" stands over against a world full of idols and rival deities. Historical understanding keeps us from turning this command into a vague encouragement to "keep God first" in a general sense; it confronts us with the demand for exclusive worship of the one true God in a world that still offers modern idols.

When Jesus delivers the Sermon on the Mount, He speaks to Jews living under Roman rule and steeped in the traditions of the scribes and Pharisees. The Beatitudes, His teaching on anger, lust, divorce, oaths, and love for enemies all strike at distortions of the law and at shallow righteousness. If we ignore that historical setting, we might turn the Sermon into a set of disconnected sayings. Seen in context, it is the King announcing the standards of His kingdom in the face of religious hypocrisy and externalism.

Historical work therefore does not pull us away from the text; it pushes us into it. It helps us hear the Spirit-inspired words with the same sharp edges they had for the first hearers.

Paying Close Attention to Grammar and Words

Words in Their Sentences and Paragraphs

The Holy Spirit chose to communicate through normal human language. That means verbs, nouns, prepositions, tenses, and sentence structure matter. The Historical-Grammatical Method insists that we pay attention to these details because meaning is carried by them.

In the opening of John's Gospel we read, "In the beginning was the Word, and the Word was with God, and the Word was God." The repeated "was" points to continuous existence; the Word did not come into being at the beginning but already was. "With God" uses language of personal relationship, not mere proximity. "The Word was God" affirms full deity. These observations are not mystical insights; they are simple grammatical realities.

Likewise, when Paul writes in Romans that all "have sinned and fall short of the glory of God," the present tense "fall short" shows an ongoing condition, not a single isolated failure. Language matters because God chose to reveal truth through sentences, not through loose slogans.

Word Meanings in Real Contexts

The Historical-Grammatical Method also insists that words are defined by usage, not by importing later theological vocabulary back into earlier texts or by choosing whichever meaning suits our system.

For example, the word "justify" in Paul's letters is a legal term meaning to declare righteous, not to make inwardly righteous. That becomes clear when we follow how Paul uses the term in Romans and Galatians. When some interpreters redefine the word to fit their own theological explanations, they are no longer practicing grammatical-historical exegesis; they are bending the text to their own scheme.

The same applies to expressions related to the Holy Spirit. Phrases such as "the Spirit dwells in you" or "you are a temple of the Holy Spirit" must be understood by examining how Paul uses "dwells," "temple," and similar language in the surrounding context. As we saw in earlier chapters, these expressions describe relationship, ownership, and guidance through the Spirit-inspired Word, not a mystical, bodily occupancy. The Historical-Grammatical Method protects us from reading later charismatic ideas back into the first-century text.

Recognizing Literary Genre

Different Kinds of Writing, Different Expectations

The Bible is one book with many kinds of writing. Law, narrative, proverb, psalm, prophecy, parable, letter, and apocalyptic vision each have patterns that must be respected. The Historical-Grammatical Method pays attention to those patterns so that we neither flatten them all into the same thing nor treat them as if they were free for imaginative allegory.

Narrative recounts events in time. Proverbs give general observations of how life normally works, not absolute promises in every situation. Poetry intensifies truth through imagery and parallel lines. Prophecy often mingles near and far events and frequently uses symbolic language. Letters apply doctrine to concrete congregational situations. Apocalyptic literature (such as parts of Daniel and Revelation) uses vivid symbols to unveil God's purposes and the certain defeat of evil.

Examples of Genre Sensitivity

When Psalm 23 says, "Jehovah is my shepherd; I shall not want," the Historical-Grammatical Method recognizes a metaphor. The psalmist is not claiming to be a literal sheep, and Jehovah is not literally holding a staff. The imagery conveys protection, provision, and guidance. The meaning is real and rich, but it is not woodenly literal.

When Jesus tells the parable of the Good Samaritan, He is not providing a historical report of a specific man on a specific road whose name we must find in some record. He is pressing His hearers to rethink who counts as a "neighbor." The Historical-Grammatical Method asks what this parable meant in that discussion between Jesus and the lawyer, then draws application from the meaning, not from hidden symbolic correspondences in every detail.

Genre awareness also guards us against misusing apocalyptic imagery. When Revelation describes beasts, horns, and bowls, the point is not to decode each number as if Scripture were a secret puzzle book. The point is to see, in symbolic form, the certainty that human empires opposed to God will fall and that the Lamb will triumph.

Staying Within the Canonical and Immediate Context

Scripture Interprets Scripture

Because the Holy Spirit is the ultimate Author of all Scripture, the Bible does not contradict itself. The Historical-Grammatical Method therefore gives priority to the immediate context, then to the context of the book, and finally to the rest of the canon. Clear passages help us interpret those that are more compressed or difficult.

For example, when we read in James that a person is "justified by works and not by faith alone," we must not wrench that sentence away from James's concern with empty claims of faith that show no obedience. Nor may we tear it away from Paul's extended explanation that justification before God is by faith apart from works of law. The same Spirit inspired both men. James confronts a dead, word-only "faith"; Paul confronts reliance on law-keeping. When read in context, they stand together.

Guarding Against Private Interpretations

Peter warns that "no prophecy of Scripture comes from someone's own interpretation." In context he speaks about the origin of prophecy, but his warning also undercuts the notion that individuals may load a passage with meanings that arise from their imagination rather than from the inspired text. The Historical-Grammatical Method is a deliberate refusal to treat Scripture as wax that can be molded into any shape.

This has direct application to texts about the Holy Spirit. When some read Romans 8 or John 14–16 as if they were primarily written to modern individuals promising inner voices and subjective impressions, they have ignored the immediate context, the original audience, and the purpose of those chapters. Those passages are anchored in the apostolic mission and in the Spirit's work through the completed revelation. The Historical-Grammatical Method pulls us back to those anchors.

Why We Reject the Historical-Critical Method

The Historical-Grammatical Method is not the only way people have approached Scripture. For more than a century, an alternative cluster of approaches has often been grouped under the label "historical-critical." These approaches typically begin with the assumption that the Bible is a purely human product that must be tested and corrected by modern thought. Source criticism, form criticism, and redaction criticism ask how texts might have been assembled from earlier writings, oral forms, or editorial layers.

At first glance this may sound scholarly and harmless, but the underlying spirit is very different from reverent exegesis. Instead of letting Scripture interpret Scripture, the critic sits over the text as judge. The text's claims about authorship, miracles, and prophecy are treated with suspicion. Predictions are re-dated after the events. Passages that speak with full divine authority are reinterpreted as the evolving religious consciousness of Israel or the church.

Because we are committed to the Bible as the Spirit-breathed, fully inerrant Word of God, we cannot accept a method that starts by doubting what Scripture says about itself. Historical information, archaeology, and linguistic study are valuable servants, but when they are used to overturn clear biblical claims, the servant has tried to become the master. The Historical-Grammatical Method gladly uses every sound fact that helps us understand the world of the text, but it will not submit the text to theories that contradict the Spirit's own testimony.

Basic Movements in Historical-Grammatical Interpretation

Even though we avoid turning Bible study into a mechanical checklist, it is helpful to describe the normal movements involved in this method.

A careful reader begins by observing the passage repeatedly, in its context, until the flow of thought becomes familiar. Questions arise: Who is speaking? To whom? About what? Why now?

Next comes closer study of the words and grammar. Key terms are traced through the book. Verb tenses and sentence connections are noticed. Cause and effect, contrasts, and parallels are marked.

The historical setting is then considered more fully. What do we know from Scripture itself about the situation? How do other passages shed light on this one? Where extra-biblical historical data is available and reliable, it may clarify customs, geography, or political realities, but it never overturns what the text plainly states.

Literary form is weighed. Is this law, psalm, parable, or letter? How does that shape the way the message is communicated?

Only after these steps are we ready to summarize what the author meant. Application flows from that meaning, not from our feelings or modern questions. The same Spirit who once moved the writer now presses that original, Spirit-given message onto our hearts and lives.

Examples of the Method at Work

Genesis 1 and the Days of Creation

When we approach Genesis 1 historically and grammatically, we are not free to treat it as a myth or as pure poetry, nor must we force it into a modern scientific scheme. The chapter presents a real beginning of the heavens and the earth by the one true God. The repeated "And God said" emphasizes that creation is by His Word. The term "day" is connected with "evening and morning," yet Scripture itself later uses "day" for extended periods. Within the overall teaching of Scripture, it is clear that the "days" mark ordered stages in God's creative work rather than rigid twenty-four-hour slices measured by a physical sun that is not even mentioned until the fourth "day."

The Historical-Grammatical Method allows the text to define its own terms within the whole canon instead of forcing it to match either modern naturalism or speculative chronologies.

Romans 8 and Life in the Spirit

Romans 8 is frequently quoted to support a mystical notion of the Holy Spirit quietly whispering inside the believer. A grammatical-historical reading restrains such claims. Paul contrasts "in the flesh" with "in the Spirit." To be "in the flesh" is to be under the rule of sin and death; to be "in the Spirit" is to belong to Christ and to live under the new rule of the gospel.

When he says, "If the Spirit of him who raised Jesus from the dead dwells in you...," he uses relational and covenant language already prepared by the Old Testament. Jehovah "dwelt" in the midst of Israel when His presence was associated with the tabernacle; yet He was not locked inside a building. His dwelling described His favor, rule, and accessibility. In the same way, the Spirit "dwells" in believers by establishing ownership, control, and guidance through the truth He has revealed. Romans 8:11 promises future bodily resurrection to those who belong to Christ; it does not teach that the Spirit is literally, physically located inside the chest of each Christian as a kind of separate spiritual entity.

The Historical-Grammatical Method therefore protects us from loading Paul's words with later charismatic assumptions. It keeps the focus on what Paul actually argues: that those who submit to the gospel live in a new realm, shaped and governed by the Spirit's revelation.

John 14–16 and the Promise of the Helper

Jesus' Upper Room discourse is another place where interpretation often goes astray. Many readers treat these chapters as if they were mainly about the Spirit giving private impressions to every believer in every age. But the historical and grammatical setting makes it clear that Jesus is speaking first of all to the apostles as chosen witnesses.

He tells *them* that the Helper will teach *them all things*, remind *them of all that He said*, and guide *them into all the truth*. That is the language of foundational revelation. The Spirit's ministry here is directly connected with the production of the New Testament, not with ongoing extra-biblical revelations for every Christian.

When we apply the Historical-Grammatical Method, we still recognize that the Spirit uses those very words to comfort and strengthen believers today. Yet we understand that He does so through the completed apostolic testimony, not by bypassing it. The same chapters that some use to justify subjective impressions actually exalt the sufficiency of the Spirit-inspired Word.

The Holy Spirit and the Historical-Grammatical Method

Some people mistakenly suggest that a careful, text-centered approach to Scripture somehow leaves out the Holy Spirit, as if reverent study were a substitute for spiritual dependence. In reality, the opposite is true. To abandon the Historical-Grammatical Method in favor of allegory, codes, or inner impressions is to act as though the Spirit did not do His work well when He inspired the text.

The Holy Spirit's own method of guiding the church is bound up with the words He breathed out. He does not apologize for using grammar, history, and genre. He chose them. When we refuse to do the hard work of understanding those things, we are not being more spiritual; we are neglecting the very instrument He has given.

This is why believers must resist both cold intellectualism and undisciplined subjectivity. Cold intellectualism treats the Bible only as a field for analysis without worship or obedience. Undisciplined subjectivity treats the Bible as raw material for personal impressions. The Historical-Grammatical Method, practiced with humility, avoids both extremes. It leads us to listen carefully, think clearly, and submit fully.

As we keep coming back to the text, seeking the author's intended meaning in its real historical setting, paying close attention to the words and structure, honoring the genre, and letting Scripture interpret Scripture, we are not merely handling ancient literature. We are listening to the Holy Spirit speaking in the very words He chose. That is the heart of the Historical-Grammatical Method and the only safe path for those who confess the Bible as the Spirit-breathed, inerrant, and sufficient Word of the living God.

CHAPTER 15 Introduction to Conservative Biblical Exegesis

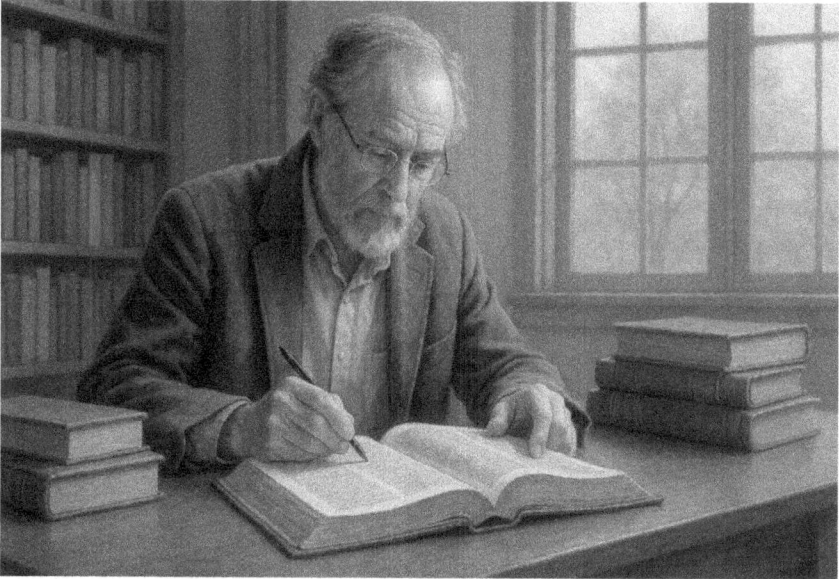

The Authority and Inerrancy of Scripture

Conservative biblical exegesis begins with a settled conviction: Scripture is the very Word of God, truthful in all that it affirms and therefore absolutely authoritative. Paul writes, "All Scripture is inspired by God and profitable for teaching, for reproof, for correction, for training in righteousness; so that the man of God may be fully competent, equipped for every good work" (2 Timothy 3:16–17). If every part of Scripture is God-breathed and sufficient to equip the believer for "every good work," then no other authority can stand above it—neither church tradition, nor academic fashion, nor private religious experience.

Conservative exegesis therefore approaches the Bible not as raw material to be reshaped by modern theory, but as a finished, inerrant revelation to be understood and obeyed. The task of the interpreter is to discover what God has said through the human authors, not to decide what He should have said.

This immediately sets conservative exegesis over against liberal-moderate criticism, which routinely questions the reliability, unity, and divine authority of Scripture. Where such criticism treats the Bible as a fallible human book to be dissected and corrected, conservative exegesis receives it as the inerrant Word of God, whose meaning must be carefully uncovered and faithfully proclaimed.

Conservative Exegesis and the Historical-Grammatical Method

The central tool of conservative exegesis is the historical-grammatical method. This is not an exotic technique but a disciplined way of reading that asks three simple questions:

1. **What did this text mean in its original historical situation?**

2. **How do the words and grammar actually work in the sentence?**

3. **What kind of writing (genre) am I dealing with?**

The goal is always the same: to arrive at the author's intended meaning as the original readers would have understood it. Only after that work is done can we make valid application to today.

This method is not neutral. It is rooted in the conviction that the same God who inspired Scripture also placed it in real history, in real languages, and in real literary forms. Because He chose to reveal

Himself in that way, we honor Him by taking history, grammar, and genre seriously.

Historical Context: Hearing the Text in Its Own World

Conservative exegesis insists that a text cannot be rightly interpreted if it is ripped out of its historical setting. God did not deliver Scripture as a timeless stack of abstract propositions; He spoke in specific times, cultures, and situations.

When Isaiah records, "In the year that King Uzziah died I saw the Lord sitting upon a throne, high and lifted up" (Isaiah 6:1), that date is not a decorative detail. Uzziah's death marked a moment of political uncertainty and moral decay in Judah. Isaiah's vision of Jehovah's holiness and sovereign rule comes in the middle of national instability. A conservative interpreter therefore asks:

- What was happening in Judah at that time?
- How would Isaiah's contemporaries have heard this vision?
- How does the historical crisis sharpen the force of the call, "Whom shall I send, and who will go for us?"

The same principle applies to New Testament letters. Romans, for example, was written to a mixed community of Jewish and Gentile believers in the capital of the Empire. Tensions about the Law, circumcision, and the place of Israel are everywhere in the background. When Paul says, "For I am not ashamed of the gospel, for it is the power of God for salvation to everyone who believes, to the Jew first and also to the Greek" (Romans 1:16), a conservative exegete hears that sentence against the background of real ethnic tensions and real questions about how Jews and Gentiles stand before God on equal footing.

Without historical context, interpretation slides quickly into imagination. With it, we hear the text as those first hearers did.

Grammatical Analysis: Letting the Words Speak

Conservative exegesis also insists that words, tenses, and syntax matter. The Holy Spirit did not inspire vague impressions but concrete sentences in Hebrew, Aramaic, and Greek. To respect His work, we must respect how language functions.

Consider John 1:1: "In the beginning was the Word, and the Word was with God, and the Word was God." Grammatical attention shows:

- The repeated verb "was" (imperfect tense) points to continual existence. The Word did not come into being at the beginning; the Word already was.

- The phrase "the Word was with God" uses a preposition that conveys personal relationship and face-to-face nearness, not mere proximity.

- The phrase "the Word was God" asserts full deity without collapsing the distinction between the Word and God mentioned just before.

A conservative interpreter does not rush past these details. He recognizes that the doctrine of Christ's eternal deity rests, in part, on careful, grammatical reading of this verse and others like it.

In the same way, careless or agenda-driven handling of grammar can distort doctrine. For example, statements about the Spirit "dwelling in" believers (such as Romans 8:9–11; 1 Corinthians 3:16; 6:19) are often wrenched from context and pressed into service of a mystical, quasi-automatic "indwelling" doctrine detached from the

Spirit's own chosen instrument: the inspired Word. A conservative, historical-grammatical reading keeps Paul's argument intact: he contrasts a fleshly mindset with a Spirit-governed, Word-shaped mindset, and he anchors believers' future bodily resurrection in the same divine power that raised Christ. The passage offers no support for modern charismatic notions of an inner voice or ongoing, extra-biblical impressions.

In other words, grammar guards us from reading into the text what we want to find there.

Literary Genre: Reading Each Text as It Was Written

The Bible is not one flat genre. It contains law codes, narratives, psalms, wisdom sayings, prophetic oracles, parables, letters, and apocalyptic visions. Conservative exegesis takes those differences seriously.

- A **psalm** frequently uses poetry, parallelism, and vivid imagery. "Jehovah is my shepherd; I shall not want" (Psalm 23:1) is not teaching that God literally carries a staff and tends literal sheep. The genre signals metaphor from the start.

- A **parable** is a story with a point, not a puzzle inviting us to assign symbolic meaning to every detail. In the parable of the Good Samaritan, the main thrust is clear: "Go, and do likewise" (Luke 10:37).

- **Apocalyptic** passages, such as parts of Daniel or Revelation, are saturated with symbols. A conservative interpreter does not flatten those symbols into newspaper-level predictions, but neither does he dissolve them into mystical vagueness. He allows the genre itself to shape what "literal" faithfulness looks like in each case.

Conservative exegesis refuses to treat poetry as if it were a lab report or to read parables as if they were coded historical chronologies. Genre sensitivity guards us both from naïve literalism and from liberal allegorizing that dissolves concrete meaning.

Why Conservative Exegesis Rejects Modern Critical Approaches

Modern biblical criticism operates under a very different set of assumptions. Even when technical tools overlap (word studies, historical research, attention to genre), liberal-moderate approaches often proceed as if:

- Scripture is fundamentally a human product,

- the text is riddled with error, contradiction, and confusion, and

- the interpreter stands as judge over the text.

Conservative exegesis exposes several core problems in these approaches.

Historical Criticism and Fragmented Scripture

Historical criticism often treats biblical books as anonymous compilations of conflicting traditions, stitched together by unknown redactors. The Pentateuch becomes a patchwork of sources; the Gospels become competing community narratives; the letters of Paul are sorted into "authentic," "disputed," and "pseudonymous" piles based on shifting scholarly fashions.

The result is a Bible with no coherent voice, no unified Author, and no stable authority. Conservative exegesis resists this fragmentation. It takes seriously what the books claim about themselves (for example, Mosaic authorship of the Law, Pauline authorship of the letters that bear his name) unless there are overwhelming textual reasons to conclude otherwise. It recognizes that the Holy Spirit can superintend real historical processes without producing chaos or contradiction.

Form and Redaction Criticism: Speculation Without Evidence

Form criticism and redaction criticism seek to peel back layers of supposed oral tradition and editorial shaping behind the canonical text. The Gospels, for instance, are reimagined as collections of small units that floated in the life of the church for decades before being stitched together. The supposed "prehistory" of these units is then reconstructed with very little hard evidence.

Conservative exegesis notes that such reconstructions are largely speculative and often driven by philosophical commitments rather than by the actual text. The canonical form of Scripture is treated as a problem to be solved instead of the God-given object of interpretation. Rather than chasing hypothetical earlier forms, conservative exegesis concentrates on the inspired form we actually possess.

Literary and Postmodern Approaches Detached from Truth

Some modern literary approaches focus almost exclusively on how a text "functions" for readers, while postmodern theories treat meaning as open-ended and endlessly negotiable. In practice, this can mean that the authority of the text is replaced by the creativity of the interpreter.

Conservative exegesis refuses that move. While it gladly uses sound literary observations (structure, repetition, themes), it insists that the biblical text has a real, determinate meaning rooted in the author's intent and in God's own purpose. The question is not, "What can this text be made to mean?" but "What did God say here, and how must I respond?"

Core Theological Commitments Underlying Conservative Exegesis

Conservative exegesis is not a bare technique; it rests on clear theological commitments.

Scripture's Authority

Because men "spoke from God as they were carried along by the Holy Spirit" (2 Peter 1:21), the Bible carries God's own authority. Conservative exegesis therefore refuses to place any external standard over Scripture—whether academic consensus, cultural sensibilities, or church tradition. Everything else must be tested by the Word, not the other way around.

Scripture's Clarity

The essential message of Scripture is clear enough that ordinary believers, using ordinary means, can understand what God requires. Psalm 119:105 says, "Your word is a lamp to my feet and a light to my path." Conservative exegesis does not pretend that all texts are equally easy, but it rejects the idea that only a guild of specialists can know what God has said. The historical-grammatical method is simply careful common sense applied with reverence.

Scripture's Sufficiency

Because all Scripture is God-breathed and profitable "so that the man of God may be fully competent, equipped for every good work"

(2 Timothy 3:16–17), the Bible is sufficient for faith and life. Conservative exegesis therefore does not chase fresh revelations, inner whispers, or mystical impressions. It sees such pursuits as undermining the Spirit's own work in the inspired text. Claims about the "indwelling" Spirit that move beyond or against Scripture are not signs of deeper spirituality; they are signs of drifting from sufficiency.

Practical Shape of Conservative Exegesis

These convictions must translate into habits. Conservative exegesis shapes how believers study, teach, and defend Scripture in daily practice.

For Personal Bible Study

A conservative, historical-grammatical approach to personal study involves:

1. **Context First:** Read the paragraph, chapter, and book, not stray verses ripped out of place.

2. **Historical Awareness:** Use good tools (introductions, atlases, background works) to understand the setting, but never let speculative theories overturn the plain sense of the text.

3. **Grammatical Attention:** Notice repeated words, commands, contrasts, conjunctions ("for," "therefore," "but"), and the flow of the argument.

4. **Genre Sensitivity:** Read psalms as poetry, proverbs as general wisdom sayings, parables as illustrative stories with main points, and letters as carefully argued instruction.

When a verse like Romans 8:11 is studied in that way, the reader is guarded from mystical misreadings. He sees that Paul is grounding the believer's future bodily resurrection in the objective historical fact of Christ's resurrection and in the same divine power that worked in Christ—not teaching a mysterious, inner, extra-biblical voice of the Spirit.

For Teaching and Preaching

In the pulpit and classroom, conservative exegesis commits to:

- preach the text in context,

- explain what the author meant before applying it,

- resist the temptation to twist passages to fit current trends (whether charismatic, psychological, or academic), and

- let Scripture critique our systems rather than forcing Scripture under them.

A sermon on the Beatitudes, for example, must first clarify what "poor in spirit" meant in Jesus' setting and how those hearers would have understood "the kingdom of heaven," before attempting to draw modern applications.

For Theological Construction

When developing doctrine—on the Holy Spirit, justification, sanctification, or anything else—conservative exegesis:

- gathers all relevant texts,

- interprets each historically and grammatically,

- allows clearer passages to shed light on more difficult ones, and

- refuses to build doctrines on obscure phrases or disputed readings.

This disciplined method is precisely what keeps a work on the Holy Spirit from sliding into the errors of literal "indwelling," ongoing revelation, or the idea that God sends trials as deliberate personal tests. Instead, doctrine is anchored in carefully interpreted texts that speak plainly when read in their own context.

Exposing the Biases Behind Modern Criticism

Conservative exegesis also pulls back the curtain on the philosophical currents driving much modern critical work. Many "neutral" methods rest on assumptions such as:

- **Secular humanism:** Human reason is the final authority; therefore, miracles and prophecy must be re-interpreted or explained away.

- **Enlightenment skepticism:** Ancient texts are guilty until proven innocent; traditional attributions of authorship or unity are treated with suspicion by default.

- **Idealist and postmodern philosophies:** The interpreter's consciousness or community shapes reality; therefore, meaning is fluid and open-ended.

Once these assumptions are exposed, it becomes clear why modern criticism so often attacks the authority, coherence, and inerrancy of Scripture. Conservative exegesis refuses these foundations outright. It is not impressed by the aura of "scholarship" when that scholarship is built on a worldview that denies or marginalizes God's self-revelation.

Conservative Exegesis as Protection and Provision

In the end, conservative biblical exegesis is both a shield and a gift.

- **As a shield**, it protects the church from fashionable but destructive errors—whether liberal denials of inerrancy, speculative reconstructions of the text's "prehistory," or popular spiritualities that claim the Holy Spirit still speaks apart from the written Word.

- **As a gift**, it provides believers with a clear, disciplined, God-honoring way to hear what He has actually said in Scripture and to build their lives on that unshakable foundation.

To interpret the Bible conservatively, then, is not to be stubbornly traditional for its own sake. It is to take seriously that Jehovah has spoken, that His Spirit has breathed out an inerrant Word, and that our proper place is not over that Word as judges, but under it as grateful hearers and obedient servants.

APPENDIX A Is Speaking in Tongues a Biblical Teaching?

Tongues and the Question We Must Really Answer

Speaking in tongues is not just a curiosity; for many it has become a test of whether a Christian is "Spirit-filled" or truly has the Holy Spirit. That makes it vital to ask not, "What have I seen or felt?" but, "What does Scripture actually teach when it is read carefully, historically, and grammatically?" If the Bible is the fully inspired, inerrant Word of God, then experience must be tested by Scripture, not Scripture reshaped by experience.

When we approach the New Testament with that conviction, a consistent picture emerges. Tongues were real human languages, given for a limited purpose in the apostolic age, as a sign to unbelievers and as part of the foundational, once-for-all work of the Holy Spirit in launching the church and confirming new revelation. That picture does not match most modern charismatic claims.

Tongues at Pentecost: Real Languages, Not Ecstatic Sounds

The first appearance of tongues is on the Day of Pentecost. Luke's description is precise and historical, not mystical and vague:

"And they were all filled with the Holy Spirit and began to speak with other tongues, as the Spirit was giving them utterance. Now there were Jews living in Jerusalem, devout men from every nation under heaven. And when this sound occurred, the multitude came together, and they were bewildered because each one of them was hearing them speak in his own language." (Acts 2:4–6)

Luke immediately explains what "other tongues" means: each listener hears the apostles "in his own language." A few verses later he even lists the regions represented and says, "we hear them in our own tongues speaking of the mighty deeds of God" (Acts 2:11).

There is nothing here of unintelligible syllables or private ecstatic speech. The miracle lies in the fact that ordinary Galileans suddenly proclaim the works of God in dozens of genuine languages they never learned, and the crowd recognizes those languages as their own. In other words, tongues at Pentecost are real, identifiable human languages used to communicate real content.

The Purpose of Tongues: A Sign Bound to the Apostolic Mission

Jesus had prepared the apostles for this moment. Just before His ascension He promised, "You will receive power when the Holy Spirit has come upon you; and you will be my witnesses in Jerusalem and in all Judea and Samaria, and to the end of the earth" (Acts 1:8). Pentecost is the first great public proof that His promise has begun to be fulfilled.

Tongues at Pentecost serve at least three clear purposes. First, they mark that the promised Holy Spirit has been poured out from the exalted Christ. Second, they signal that the gospel is now aimed at "every nation under heaven," not just one people. Third, they authenticate the apostles as God's chosen messengers for this new era.

Later, Paul explains that tongues are "a sign, not to those who believe but to unbelievers" (1 Corinthians 14:22). Drawing on Isaiah's warning that Jehovah would speak to His disobedient people "by men of strange tongues," Paul shows that foreign languages function as a striking sign of God's activity and of judgment on unbelief. The emphasis is again public, objective, and evangelistic, not private and mystical.

Scripture never presents tongues as a required proof of salvation, a universal badge of a "second blessing," or a normal prayer language that all Christians should seek. On the contrary, Paul asks, "All do not speak with tongues, do they?" (1 Corinthians 12:30), with the obvious answer, "No."

Tongues in Corinth: A Real Gift That Needed Restraint

The Corinthian church did experience the genuine gift of tongues, yet it quickly turned that gift into a badge of status and a source of disorder. That is why 1 Corinthians 12–14 contains the most detailed teaching on tongues in the New Testament.

Paul never denies that tongues are a real gift. He thanks God that he speaks in tongues more than all of them (1 Corinthians 14:18). But he insists that the gift must be governed by the larger principle that the church is to be edified through clear, intelligible teaching. Speaking "in a tongue" without interpretation may be prayer to God, but it does not build up others, because they cannot understand what is being said (1 Corinthians 14:2–4).

For that reason Paul sets strict limits. If tongues are used in the assembly, there must be interpretation; otherwise the speaker is to remain silent in the congregation and speak to himself and to God (1 Corinthians 14:27–28). At most two or three may speak in tongues, and always one at a time, never in a chaotic mass. Everything is to be done "decently and in order" (1 Corinthians 14:40).

It is important to see that these regulations presuppose the same basic nature of tongues that Acts 2 displays. Paul can talk about interpretation because there is a real message in a real language that can be rendered into another language. The gift is not an outpouring of random sounds with no linguistic structure.

"When the Perfect Comes": Tongues as a Temporary, Foundational Gift

In the midst of correcting Corinth, Paul places tongues and other miraculous gifts in a larger time-frame. He writes,

"Love never fails; but if there are gifts of prophecy, they will be done away; if there are tongues, they will cease; if there is knowledge, it will be done away. For we know in part and we prophesy in part; but when the perfect comes, the partial will be done away." (1 Corinthians 13:8–10)

The "partial" here is the fragmentary, developing revelatory situation of the apostolic age. Prophecy, tongues, and special knowledge are all linked as temporary means by which Jehovah supplied guidance to a church that did not yet possess the completed New Testament. The "perfect" is not heaven in the abstract but the state in which the church possesses the full, mature revelation of the gospel in written, Spirit-breathed form.

Once that "perfect" revelation had been given and preserved in the inspired Scriptures, those partial, sign-gifts had served their purpose. They were never presented as permanent features of ordinary church life across the centuries. Instead, they belong to the foundation stage, just as apostles and New Testament prophets themselves do (Ephesians 2:20).

The Witness of Early Church History

The pattern of church history matches this biblical expectation. After the age of the apostles, clear references to genuine, New Testament-type tongues rapidly diminish. Early post-apostolic writers speak at length about doctrine, persecution, baptism, the Lord's Supper, and church order, but tongues as described in Acts 2 and 1 Corinthians 12–14 are not presented as a normal, ongoing experience for the ordinary congregation.

Where later claims of "tongues" appear in fringe groups, they are often associated with fanaticism, doctrinal deviation, or disorder rather than with sober, apostolic Christianity. That does not prove everything by itself, but it does harmonize with Scripture's own signal that tongues and similar sign-gifts would fade once their foundational role was complete.

Evaluating Modern Tongues by the Biblical Standard

Modern Pentecostal and Charismatic movements claim that speaking in tongues has returned as a normal mark of Spirit-baptism or deeper Christian life. However, when we test these claims by the biblical record, several serious gaps appear.

First, the nature of the speech is different. New Testament tongues are real human languages. Most modern "tongues" are acknowledged even by sympathetic researchers to be non-linguistic, consisting of repeated syllables and sounds that do not match any identifiable language.

Second, the purpose is different. In the New Testament, tongues function as a sign to unbelievers and as part of the public confirmation of new revelation. Today, tongues are often promoted for private edification, emotional release, or as a personal proof that one has received the Holy Spirit. That is exactly the kind of individualistic, inward focus that Paul corrects in Corinth.

Third, the practice is different. Paul requires strict order, limited numbers, and mandatory interpretation in the assembly. In many modern gatherings, groups speak at once, no interpretation is given, and confusion rather than edification results. Whatever else may be happening, it is not submission to the apostolic pattern.

Fourth, the timeline is different. Scripture indicates that tongues were part of the "partial" revelatory phase and would cease when "the perfect" came, whereas modern teaching often insists that tongues should be a permanent, universal sign until the end of the age.

When a practice differs from Scripture in its nature, purpose, practice, and time-frame, a conservative, historical-grammatical reading of the Bible cannot call that practice "the biblical gift of tongues."

The Holy Spirit Today: Not Less Present, but Differently at Work

To say that the miraculous gift of tongues has ceased is not to say that the Holy Spirit is absent or powerless today. It is to say that He now works in the way He Himself promised for the post-apostolic church: through the completed, inspired Scriptures. All Scripture is "inspired by God" and is sufficient to equip the man of God "for every good work" (2 Timothy 3:16–17).

The Spirit who once confirmed new revelation with signs now confirms that completed revelation by opening minds and hearts to understand, believe, and obey it. He convicts the world of sin, righteousness, and judgment through the gospel message. He regenerates through the "living and abiding word of God" (1 Peter 1:23). He sanctifies through the truth of the Word. He comforts, assures, and strengthens believers as they take that Word into their minds and live it out in their lives.

A church that has the full New Testament and yet chases after new tongues, new revelations, and new signs is like a person who leaves a strong lamp on the table and goes searching in the dark for candles. The present work of the Holy Spirit is not less real because it is tied to the Bible; it is more secure and more available, because every believer can open the same Spirit-given, inerrant Word.

Conclusion: Honoring the Spirit by Honoring His Word

Speaking in tongues was indeed a biblical teaching and a real gift in the first century. It was miraculous, intelligible, and purposeful. It served as a sign to unbelievers, a tool for rapid proclamation, and a confirmation of the new apostolic revelation at the birth of the church. But Scripture itself tells us that this gift was part of the "partial" and would cease when the "perfect" came.

Modern practices that go by the name "tongues" do not match the New Testament description in content, purpose, or order, and they are not needed in an age when the Holy Spirit has already given the church the complete, written, all-sufficient Word of God. To honor the Holy Spirit is not to seek a revival of temporary sign-gifts but to submit humbly, joyfully, and reverently to the Scriptures He has breathed out, trusting that through that Word He still does His deep and powerful work in the hearts of those who believe.

APPENDIX B Is Snake Handling Biblical?

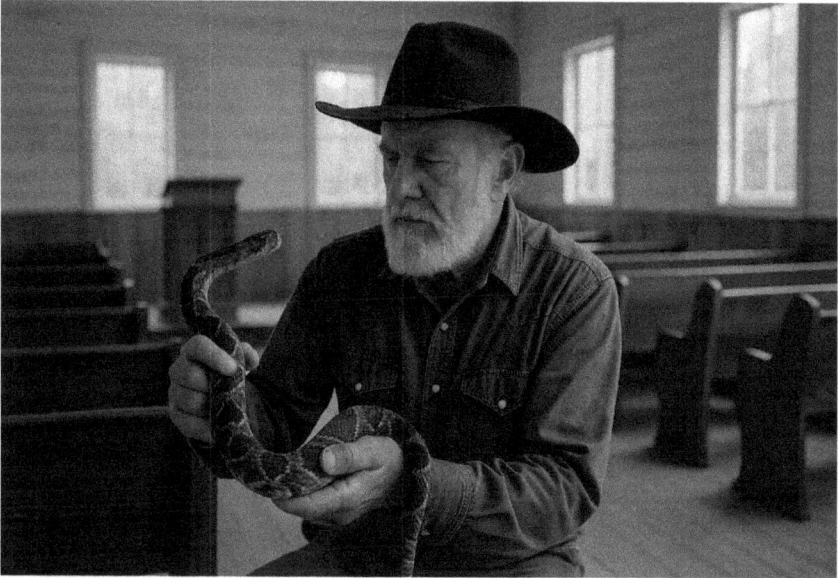

The practice of snake handling, sometimes called serpent handling, is a fringe ritual found in a small number of Pentecostal and Holiness churches in rural parts of the United States, especially in the Appalachian region. It arose in the early twentieth century and has never been more than a marginal phenomenon, but it claims biblical support and is often defended as a test or proof of faith. If we apply a conservative, historical-grammatical reading of Scripture, however, it becomes clear that snake handling is a dangerous distortion rather than an expression of genuine New Testament Christianity.

Edward D. Andrews

Historical Background of Snake Handling

Modern snake handling is generally traced to George Went Hensley (1880–1955). Around 1910 he began introducing snakes into the worship of a Holiness group in the mountains of Tennessee, arguing that true believers must "take up serpents" as a sign of salvation. Hensley eventually left the Church of God Holiness and formed independent congregations where handling venomous snakes became a required mark of obedience for those who wanted to be considered faithful.

From those beginnings, related churches appeared in scattered communities across Appalachia and the rural South. Services were often held in homes or simple meeting houses. Dress codes tended to be strict: women with uncut hair, long dresses, no make-up; men with short hair, long sleeves, and strong preaching against tobacco and alcohol. In addition to handling snakes, some groups added the deliberate drinking of poison, again appealing to certain words in Mark 16.

Despite the rhetoric of "divine protection," the history of the movement is filled with tragic deaths. Hensley himself died from a snake bite in 1955. Later well-known handlers, such as John Wayne "Punkin" Brown and Pastor Mack Wolford, likewise died after rattlesnake bites suffered in the middle of religious services. Leaders often bear scars from multiple bites, living evidence that whatever is happening, it is not a permanent, guaranteed immunity.

Passages Used to Justify Snake Handling

Snake-handling advocates commonly appeal to three passages.

First is the long ending of Mark:

"These signs will accompany those who believe: in my name they will cast out demons; they will speak with new tongues; they will pick up serpents; and if they drink any deadly poison, it will not hurt them; they will lay hands on the sick, and they will recover." (Mark 16:17–18)

Second is Jesus' statement to the seventy:

"Behold, I have given you authority to tread on serpents and scorpions, and over all the power of the enemy, and nothing will injure you." (Luke 10:19)

Third is the narrative about Paul on Malta:

"However, when Paul had gathered a bundle of sticks and laid them on the fire, a viper came out because of the heat and fastened on his hand. When the natives saw the creature hanging from his hand, they began saying to one another, 'Undoubtedly this man is a murderer, and though he has been saved from the sea, Justice has not allowed him to live.' However he shook the creature off into the fire and suffered no harm." (Acts 28:3–5)

A careful, context-sensitive reading shows that none of these texts authorizes modern believers to seek out snakes as a ritual of faith.

The Textual Problem with Mark 16:17–18

The first and most basic issue with using Mark 16:17–18 as a foundation for snake handling is textual. The Gospel of Mark almost certainly ends at 16:8 in the earliest and best Greek manuscripts. Verses 9–20, which include the promise about picking up serpents and drinking poison, are absent from the two oldest complete copies of the New Testament and from several other early witnesses. Ancient writers like Eusebius and Jerome explicitly note that the longer ending was missing from most manuscripts known to them.

In addition to this external evidence, the vocabulary and style of Mark 16:9–20 differ noticeably from the rest of the Gospel. The passage feels like a summary patch, drawing together traditions from other Gospels and early Christian teaching. Even many conservative scholars who hold firmly to inerrancy acknowledge that these verses are a later addition, not part of Mark's original composition.

This does not mean every statement in Mark 16:9–20 is false, but it does mean that building a mandatory ritual of handling venomous snakes on a disputed, likely non-original paragraph is reckless. Sound doctrine and practice should rest on passages whose text and meaning are clear, not on a late appendix whose authority is questionable even at the level of manuscript evidence.

Even if someone insists on treating Mark 16:9–20 as canonical, the text still does not prescribe snake handling services. It speaks of "signs" that would accompany those who believe in the period when the risen Christ was confirming the apostolic message. It does not command believers to seek out snakes or poison. The only narrative example we have that matches the description is precisely Acts 28, where protection occurs in an unexpected, involuntary encounter, not in a staged ceremony.

Luke 10:19 and Figurative Language

Luke 10 records Jesus sending out the seventy to proclaim the nearness of the kingdom with special authority over demons and disease. When they return rejoicing that even demons are subject to them in His name, Jesus responds:

"Behold, I have given you authority to tread on serpents and scorpions, and over all the power of the enemy, and nothing will injure you." (Luke 10:19)

To rip "serpents and scorpions" out of this setting and treat them as a permanent command for all believers to stomp on literal snakes is to ignore the way Jesus regularly uses symbolic language. The explanatory phrase "over all the power of the enemy" shows that He is talking about spiritual opposition, not about turning worship into a reptile show. Throughout Scripture, serpents and scorpions can function as images of danger, hostility, and satanic power. Jesus assures His commissioned messengers that the enemy will not finally thwart their mission.

Furthermore, the promise in Luke 10:19 is given to a specific group at a specific time under extraordinary conditions. It is not a general warranty that no believer will ever be harmed. The same Lord who spoke those words also warned His disciples that they would be hated, persecuted, and even killed (John 15:18–20). To turn Luke 10:19 into a blanket guarantee of physical invulnerability is to set Scripture against Scripture.

Acts 28 and Paul's Viper Encounter

In Acts 28, Paul is shipwrecked on Malta, helping gather firewood when a viper fastens on his hand. The islanders expect him to swell up or drop dead, but he simply shakes the snake into the fire and is unharmed. They conclude, wrongly but understandably, that he must be some kind of god.

Nothing in this passage suggests that Paul was engaging in a ritual test of faith. He was not proving anything to himself or to others by handling snakes; he was simply serving, and danger unexpectedly struck. The Lord chose, in that moment, to protect His servant to advance the gospel among the islanders. That is providence and apostolic-era sign, not a template for deliberately courting death in worship.

Using Acts 28 to justify modern snake handling is like using Paul's survival of shipwreck as an excuse to sail straight into hurricanes in the name of faith. The narrative shows God's mercy in an unplanned crisis, not a command to create crises.

Testing God versus Trusting God

When Satan tempted Jesus to throw Himself from the pinnacle of the temple, he even quoted Scripture:

"For it is written, 'He will give His angels orders concerning You'; and, 'On their hands they will lift You up, so that You do not strike Your foot against a stone.'" (Matthew 4:6)

Jesus responded with Scripture as well: "On the other hand, it is written, 'You shall not put the Lord your God to the test.'" (Matthew 4:7)

The parallel to snake handling is painfully obvious. To pick up a rattlesnake or copperhead during worship to "prove" faith is not an act of humble trust; it is an attempt to force God's hand. It is the same mentality Satan proposed: throw Yourself into danger and demand that God protect You because of a promise pulled from context. True faith rests on God's Word and obeys His commands in ordinary life; it does not manufacture peril in order to demand a miracle.

Jesus and the apostles did experience miraculous deliverances, but they did not parade those possibilities as stunts. Paul told Timothy to take a little wine for his stomach and frequent ailments (1 Timothy 5:23); he did not tell him to drink poison by faith. The normal pattern for Christians is prudence, prayer, and obedience, not theatrics with venomous animals.

Miraculous Signs and the Apostolic Era

The broader New Testament picture is that miraculous signs, including unusual protections, belonged especially to the foundational apostolic period. They confirmed the new revelation of Christ and authenticated the messengers whom God had sent. As the church matured and the Spirit completed the New Testament Scriptures, those temporary sign-gifts ceased to be part of the ordinary life of believers.

From earlier chapters we have already seen that the Holy Spirit now works through the completed, inerrant Word, not through ongoing displays of apostolic-level miracles. To insist that believers must still perform such signs to prove genuine faith is to misunderstand redemptive history. Snake handling ignores that shift, clinging to a sensational reading of a disputed text and neglecting the Spirit's actual emphasis today: holiness, sound doctrine, and loving obedience to Scripture.

Why Snake Handling Is Not Biblical Faith

When we bring all these strands together, the conclusion is clear. Snake handling is not a biblical command, not a pattern taught or modeled in Scripture, and not an expression of the Spirit's work in the present age. It rests on a weak textual foundation, misreads figurative language as literal, confuses providential protection with prescriptive ritual, and directly contradicts the Lord's own warning against testing God.

Christians are indeed called to present their bodies as a living sacrifice, holy and acceptable to God (Romans 12:1). That sacrifice is shown in daily obedience, self-denial, and service—not in waving vipers over one's head. Believers are urged to examine themselves to see whether they are in the faith (2 Corinthians 13:5), but the test is doctrinal fidelity and moral fruit, not whether one can survive a bite from a timber rattlesnake.

Handled with a conservative, historical-grammatical approach, Scripture gives no warrant for snake handling. Instead, it calls us away from sensational misuses of isolated texts and back to a sober, reverent submission to the whole counsel of God.

APPENDIX C Why Would the Holy Spirit Miraculously Inspire 66 Fully Inerrant Texts, and Then Allow Human Imperfection into the Copies?

The question is honest and unavoidable: if the Holy Spirit miraculously inspired sixty-six fully inerrant books, why did He not also guarantee perfect, error-free copies of those books in every age and place? If God went to the "trouble" of giving us an inerrant Bible, why not also give us an inerrant transmission of that Bible? This appendix will answer that question from a conservative, evangelical standpoint that strongly affirms verbal plenary inspiration, inerrancy of the autographs, and the sufficiency of the preserved text.

Inspiration: What God Did Once for All

The starting point must be a clear definition of inspiration. The Scriptures repeatedly affirm that the original writings were not merely religious reflections but the very words God chose to give.

Paul writes, "All Scripture is inspired by God and profitable for teaching, for reproof, for correction, for training in righteousness, so that the man of God may be fully competent, equipped for every good work" (2 Timothy 3:16–17). The phrase "inspired by God" (theopneustos) literally means "God-breathed." Scripture is not man's thoughts God happened to approve; it is God's own Word, breathed out through chosen men.

Peter says the same from another angle: "No prophecy was ever produced by the will of man, but men spoke from God as they were carried along by the Holy Spirit" (2 Peter 1:21). The human writers really spoke; their vocabulary, style, and background are visible on every page. Yet they were "carried along" by the Holy Spirit so that what they produced truly was the Word of God, not the word of man dressed up with religious language.

That is why the historic doctrine of verbal plenary inspiration has been carefully defined by conservative theologians:

Inspiration is the Holy Spirit's superintendence of the human authors so that, using their own personalities, they wrote and recorded without error the very words God intended, in the original manuscripts.

Notice two key elements. First, the result is inerrant: the autographs contain no error in anything the biblical authors affirm. Second, the focus is on the autographic text, not on every later copy.

Transmission: What God Ordinarily Does Through Providence

Once those autographs existed, a different divine work began: preservation through ordinary providence rather than continued miracle. God did not keep prophets and apostles standing in every scriptorium correcting each stroke of the pen. Instead, He allowed the Scriptures to be handled, copied, read, and passed along by ordinary believers, congregations, and scribes—sometimes highly skilled, sometimes less so.

Hand-copying inevitably introduces imperfections. Letters can be skipped, words doubled, lines dropped, marginal notes accidentally inserted into the text. None of this is a surprise to God, and none of it cancels what He did at the moment of inspiration. The fact that God inspired inerrant autographs does not logically require that He must also perform a continuous stream of copying miracles in every generation.

New Testament textual scholar Dirk Jongkind expresses the point simply: God has given us His actual words in the original writings, yet He did not obligate Himself to preserve every last detail in a way that bypasses normal history. Instead, He has given the church "abundant access" to those words through a large and rich manuscript tradition. The issue is not, "Did God fail?" but, "What means did He choose to use?"

Edward D. Andrews

How Textual Criticism Works in God's Providence

Because God allowed Scripture to be transmitted through human copying, the discipline of textual criticism became necessary. Textual criticism is not an enemy of inerrancy; rightly practiced, it is one of God's tools for recovering the exact wording of the autographs as closely as possible.

We now possess thousands of New Testament manuscripts and fragments, along with ancient translations and quotations in early Christian writers. When these witnesses are compared, differences can be seen and weighed. Most variations are obvious scribal slips: spelling differences, word order changes that do not affect meaning, or the presence or absence of an article. A small number are more substantial, but even there the evidence is usually strongly stacked in one direction.

Daniel Wallace has noted that the percentage of places where the original wording is genuinely uncertain and where a different reading would actually change the meaning in any significant way is only a tiny fraction—about a quarter of one percent of the New Testament. In other words, more than ninety-nine percent of the text is unaffected by any serious question, and in no case does a disputed reading overturn any doctrine of the faith.

God did not choose to preserve Scripture by freezing history; He preserved it by multiplying manuscripts. No single church, monastery, or region ever held a monopoly on the text. Precisely because copying was done in many places by many hands, no one scribe's mistake could permanently corrupt the entire stream. The Spirit, who once inspired the autographs, has overseen centuries of copying and comparison in such a way that the church still has, in practical terms, the very Word He originally breathed out.

Why God Did Not Give Miraculously Inerrant Copies

At this point the question becomes more practical and theological: why would God inspire perfect originals but not guarantee perfect copies in the same miraculous way? Several considerations help answer that without diminishing His wisdom or goodness.

First, God ordinarily works through means, not constant miracle. The whole pattern of Scripture shows that He regularly uses human minds, hands, and decisions, even though they are finite and fallible. He fed Israel with manna miraculously, but later fed them by rain, harvest, and labor. He raised Jesus from the dead miraculously, but spreads the news of that resurrection through very ordinary preaching and teaching. In the same way, He gave Scripture miraculously, then preserved it providentially through copying, collecting, and careful scholarship.

Second, allowing normal copying rather than perpetual miracle guards against idolatry of artifacts. If one perfectly preserved autograph of, say, Romans were still on display in a cathedral, human hearts would be tempted to venerate the parchment itself instead of submitting to the message written on it. By allowing the physical forms to wear out, be copied, shared, and sometimes lost, God keeps our focus on what He says, not on the relic that carries it.

Third, the existence of minor variations forces the church to engage Scripture thoughtfully rather than magically. God has not given His people a book to be treated as a charm. He calls us to love Him with all our heart, soul, mind, and strength. Comparing manuscripts, weighing evidence, and thinking carefully about the text is one way the church exercises that sanctified mind under the oversight of the Spirit.

Fourth, the presence of a few uncertain details highlights our dependence, not our despair. We are reminded that only God is omniscient. We do not know every microscopic detail of the original wording with absolute mathematical certainty, but we know enough, and far more than enough, to confess, preach, obey, and defend the faith. Our confidence rests in the God who spoke and preserved His Word, not in our own ability to control every letter.

Answering the Objection: "If God Did Not Preserve Every Detail, Did He Really Inspire?"

Bart Ehrman famously argued that if God wanted people to have His actual words, He would have miraculously preserved every last letter of them. Because God did not do that in a way that bypasses all variation, Ehrman concluded that He never inspired them in the first place. The conclusion does not follow.

That reasoning quietly assumes that God must do things in the manner we imagine or else He has not done them at all. But Scripture itself shows that God's ways are often different from human expectations. He promised a Messiah and sent a crucified carpenter. He promised a kingdom and began it like mustard seed. He promised to dwell with His people and sent the Spirit to work through a book, a body, and ordinary means of grace.

God did, in fact, preserve His Word, but He chose a way that honors both His sovereignty and human responsibility. He gave inspired autographs; He allowed normal copying; He multiplied manuscripts; He empowered generations of careful collation and study; and He gave His church a text that is demonstrably stable, reliable, and sufficient for every doctrine and duty of the Christian life.

The existence of minor variants says nothing against inspiration. It only tells us that God did not intend to make the physical transmission of Scripture an ongoing miracle parallel to the first giving of Scripture. The miracle was once-for-all at the point of inspiration; providence continues thereafter.

The Holy Spirit's Present Work: Illumination, Not New Inspiration

In all of this, the Holy Spirit has not withdrawn from Scripture. His role has changed in kind, not in faithfulness. He is no longer inspiring new books or dictating words to apostles and prophets. That work finished when the canon was completed. Today His special work toward believers in relation to Scripture is illumination, not new revelation.

The Spirit does not reveal new meanings hidden for centuries. He does not whisper secret messages into the heart that contradict or override the written Word. Rather, He opens blinded minds to see the glory of what is already there. He convicts of sin when the text exposes our hearts. He strengthens faith when we see the promises of God. He produces obedience when the commands of Scripture are received with humble trust.

As Norman Geisler helpfully put it, the Spirit's work is not to make the meaning of the text exist, but to make the significance of that meaning clear and compelling to those who believe. Meaning is embedded in the words as God originally breathed them out and as those words have been accurately preserved. Significance is how that meaning grips, changes, comforts, warns, and directs us in real life.

Confidence Without Illusion

So we may answer the original question this way. The Holy Spirit miraculously inspired sixty-six fully inerrant books because God willed to give a once-for-all, absolutely trustworthy revelation of Himself, His Son, His salvation, and His will. He then allowed human imperfection in the copying process because God willed to use ordinary providence, not constant miracle, to carry that revelation through history.

He did so in a way that never compromised His purpose. The inspired meaning of Scripture has been preserved with extraordinary accuracy. The church is not left in the dark, groping among corrupt texts, but stands under the clear light of a well-attested Bible. Through conservative textual criticism we can, in practical terms, recover the wording of the autographs to a degree that fully supports inerrancy of what God actually gave. And through the ongoing work of the Holy Spirit, we can understand, believe, and obey that Word today.

Our trust, therefore, is not in flawless scribes or perfect ink, but in the God who breathed out His Word, governed its transmission, and still speaks through it. He has not failed His people. He has given exactly what He intended us to have: an inerrant revelation in the autographs, a remarkably reliable text in our hands, and the Holy Spirit using that text to bring us to Christ and to conform us to His image.

APPENDIX D How Do We Grieve the Holy Spirit?

Paul's warning, "And do not grieve the Holy Spirit of God, by whom you were sealed for the day of redemption" (Ephesians 4:30), assumes something very serious: the Holy Spirit is not an impersonal force but a personal, holy, loving Divine Person whose work can be resisted, insulted, or treated lightly. To "grieve" Him is to live, speak, and think in ways that oppose what He has revealed in the inspired Scriptures. It is not a mystical feeling we somehow cause inside ourselves; it is the Bible's way of describing how our sin and stubbornness stand in direct contradiction to the Spirit's holy will made known in His Word.

The Context of Grieving the Spirit

Ephesians 4:30 does not stand alone. It sits in the middle of a very practical section where Paul is contrasting the old way of life with the new life shaped by the gospel. Just before and after the command not to grieve the Holy Spirit, Paul mentions lying, sinful anger, stealing, corrupt talk, bitterness, wrath, clamor, slander, and malice, over against truth, honest work, edifying speech, kindness, tenderheartedness, and forgiveness.

In other words, Paul does not invite us to stare inward trying to feel whether we have grieved the Spirit. He points to very concrete things: what we say, how we treat one another, whether we cling to grudges rather than forgive, whether our mouths tear down instead of build up. Whenever our conduct contradicts the moral will of God revealed in Scripture, we stand in opposition to the very Spirit who breathed out that Scripture. That contradiction is what Paul calls "grieving" Him.

When Paul adds that believers were "sealed" by the Holy Spirit for the day of redemption, he is not teaching a mystical, literal indwelling in the body of each Christian. He is reminding them that the Spirit's own revealed message—the gospel they believed, preserved for us in the inspired New Testament—marked them out as belonging to Christ and guaranteed their future redemption. To live in ways that contradict that gospel is to treat lightly the very Spirit who sealed them through that Word.

Human Imperfection, Bias, and the Spirit's Grief

Because we remain imperfect, even earnest believers can grieve the Holy Spirit without realizing it at first. A Christian may sincerely pray for guidance, ask that the Spirit lead him into truth, and then sit down with the Bible already determined not to change his position, no matter what the text says. In such a case, the problem is not that the Spirit has failed to "whisper" clearly enough inside; the problem is that the heart has quietly decided that cherished opinions outrank the written Word.

The historical-grammatical method of interpretation demands that we seek the plain, contextual meaning of the text as the original author intended. When we knowingly twist that meaning to preserve a favorite doctrine, excuse a sin, or defend a tradition, we are not merely making an academic error; we are resisting the Spirit who authored the text. That resistance is another way of grieving Him.

This can happen in many ways. A believer may rely on a biased translation or commentary even after seeing strong evidence that key passages have been mishandled. A teacher may discover that a cherished theological system does not square with the straightforward meaning of certain Scriptures and then quietly ignore those texts, or constantly "explain them away." A congregation may cling to practices that contradict the New Testament pattern, while claiming "the Spirit is leading us." In each case, the Spirit's own inspired Word is being set aside. That is not submission; it is grief.

Conduct That Grieves the Holy Spirit

Paul's language in Ephesians 4 is deliberately concrete. The Spirit is grieved when believers claim loyalty to Christ, yet allow their daily conduct to be shaped by the old way of life rather than the new.

He is grieved when falsehood replaces truth. Whenever we shade the facts, exaggerate, flatter, gossip, or deliberately conceal what another believer has a right to know, we align ourselves with the father of lies rather than with the Spirit of truth. The Spirit used the apostles to command, "Speak truth each one of you with his neighbor." To make deception a habit is to push back against that command.

He is grieved when anger is cherished instead of dealt with. Paul's warning, "Be angry, and yet do not sin; do not let the sun go down on your anger," shows that settled resentment gives the devil opportunity. When we nourish grudges, rehearse injuries, and refuse reconciliation, we not only damage relationships; we harden ourselves against the gracious call of the Spirit in Scripture to forgive as God in Christ forgave us.

He is grieved when selfishness rules our use of resources. The one who stole was not merely told to stop stealing, but to work and to share. The Spirit's pattern is not bare restraint but transformed generosity. When we hoard what we can share, or use our strength and skills only for ourselves, we refuse the Spirit-shaped pattern of honest labor and open-handed giving.

He is grieved when our mouths become instruments of decay rather than building. "Let no corrupt word proceed from your mouth, but only such a word as is good for building up." Sarcasm that wounds, insults, slander, crude joking, constant criticism, and careless words that crush fragile believers—all of these contradict the Spirit's design that our speech become a channel of grace.

He is grieved when bitterness, rage, shouting, and malice are allowed to take root in the heart. These are not mere personality quirks; they are sins that directly oppose the Spirit's work of producing love, joy, peace, patience, kindness, goodness, faithfulness, gentleness, and self-control through the Word. When we excuse such attitudes instead of repenting of them, we align ourselves against the Spirit's work.

In each case, the grief is not an abstract emotion. It is the Bible's way of saying that the Spirit does not approve of, nor bless, such conduct. He stands against it in the very Scriptures He has inspired.

Spiritual Insight and the Danger of Hardening

Ephesians 1:18 speaks of "the eyes of your heart being enlightened" so that you may know the hope of His calling. The Spirit's work through the Word is to open those eyes—to give spiritual insight, not in the sense of secret mystical information, but in the sense of a deep, obedient grasp of what Scripture plainly teaches. When that light is resisted, the result is not neutral; it is darkening.

Believers can cloud their own spiritual eyesight. Persistent refusal to act on what the Bible clearly says will gradually dull sensitivity. At first, a conscience shaped by Scripture is pricked. If that voice is repeatedly ignored, the Spirit's warning, given through the Word, is pushed away, and what once seemed unthinkable begins to seem normal. That drift is part of what it means to grieve Him.

Unbelievers, for their part, can often understand the bare content of the Bible. They may trace Paul's argument, outline a Gospel, or follow a narrative. But apart from repentance and faith, the significance of what they read appears foolish or unimportant. Their problem is not lack of brain power; it is moral and spiritual alienation from the God whose Word they are reading. The same Spirit who inspired the text also presses its claims on the heart; when those claims are rejected, the hardness deepens.

The Spirit's Present Work: Illumination, Not New Revelation

The Holy Spirit's special work in believers today is not to give new inspired messages beyond the Bible, nor to override their minds in a mechanical way, but to illuminate the significance of the Scriptures He has already given. The meaning of the text is fixed by the author's intention; the Spirit's work is to bring that meaning home to the conscience, to expose where our lives do not match, and to strengthen us to obey.

He does this through ordinary but powerful means: careful reading, reverent meditation, faithful teaching, honest self-examination, and humble submission to what is written. When we engage in these things with a teachable spirit, we cooperate with His work. When we insist that our feelings, experiences, or traditions are the final authority, and use them to silence or twist the written Word, we oppose Him.

This is why it is so crucial to separate the Spirit's true work from claims that treat Him as a private voice inside us that can contradict the Bible or bypass the need for serious study. To blame our disobedience, or our refusal to do hard interpretive work, on "the Spirit's guidance" is to misuse His name and grieve Him.

Avoiding Grief: Walking in Step With the Spirit Through the Word

If grieving the Holy Spirit means living and thinking against His revealed will, then avoiding that grief means bringing our lives into willing conformity with what He has already spoken. That does not require a mystical experience; it requires a humble, steady, Scripture-governed life.

This includes cultivating a heart that is quick to repent when Scripture exposes sin. It means letting the plain sense of the text correct our cherished opinions, even when that costs us pride or reputation. It means seeking reconciliation where we have wronged others, changing our speech patterns so that our words give grace instead of harm, and practicing kindness and forgiveness as the normal atmosphere of Christian relationships.

It also includes a disciplined approach to Bible study itself. We must refuse to read only those passages that confirm what we already think. We must be willing to trace arguments carefully, look at context, examine original words when necessary, and check our interpretations against the whole teaching of Scripture. That is not "academic coldness"; it is reverence for the Spirit's own words.

The Spirit is not grieved by believers who come to the Bible with questions, or who struggle to understand. He is grieved when we will not listen, when we refuse correction, or when we twist His words to justify what we already intended to do.

Comfort for the Sensitive Conscience

Many Christians who care about this subject are exactly the ones who most fear that they have grieved the Holy Spirit beyond repair. It is important to say plainly: the very fact that you are concerned, that you desire to honor Him and submit to His Word, is strong evidence that you have not hardened yourself to the point of hopelessness.

Grieving the Spirit is serious, but it is not the same as committing the unpardonable sin discussed in connection with blasphemy against the Spirit. Believers grieve Him often, yet He continues to call them back through the same Scriptures they have neglected or disobeyed.

His seal, given through the gospel, is not fragile. What needs to change is not His patience, but our response.

The path forward is not to sit in paralyzing fear, wondering whether some past misstep has ruined everything, but to return afresh to the Word He has inspired, confessing where we know we have resisted, and renewing our resolve to obey. The Spirit is honored, not by our endless introspection, but by our concrete, Scripture-shaped obedience.

Summary

To grieve the Holy Spirit is to live, speak, and interpret in ways that contradict the truth and holiness He has revealed in Scripture. It happens when sin is cherished instead of confessed, when bitterness is held rather than forgiveness extended, when our own ideas are defended at the expense of the Bible's plain teaching, and when we treat His inspired Word as negotiable. The remedy is not a search for new revelations or inner voices, but a humble return to the written Word, a willingness to be corrected by it, and a life that increasingly reflects the kindness, purity, and love that the Spirit produces through that Word. In this way we move from grieving Him to pleasing Him, as we are led, not by private impulses, but by the Spirit-inspired Scriptures.

APPENDIX E How Can We Cultivate the Holy Spirit

The Bible never calls Christians to "coax" the Holy Spirit down from heaven or to wait for some mystical sensation. Instead, Scripture calls believers to live in such a way that the Spirit's work through the inspired Word shapes their thoughts, desires, and habits. To "cultivate the Holy Spirit," in biblical terms, is to cultivate a life that is increasingly governed by the Spirit's teaching in Scripture rather than by the flesh.

The Biblical Foundation for Cultivating the Spirit

Paul gives us the clearest portrait of what a Spirit-governed life looks like:

"But the fruit of the Spirit is love, joy, peace, patience, kindness, goodness, faithfulness, gentleness, self-control; against such things there is no law. And those who belong to Christ Jesus have crucified the flesh with its passions and desires. If we live by the Spirit, let us also walk by the Spirit. Let us not become conceited, provoking one another, envying one another." (Gal. 5:22-26)

The "fruit of the Spirit" is not a list of feelings that appear out of nowhere. These are settled, tested qualities of character that emerge as the Spirit, through the Word, renews the mind and redirects the will. To "live by the Spirit" and to "walk by the Spirit" is to let Scripture rule what we love, how we think, and how we treat others.

Walking by the Spirit and Putting the Flesh to Death

The contrast between a Spirit-governed life and a flesh-governed life is sharply drawn in Romans:

"For those who are according to the flesh set their minds on the things of the flesh, but those who are according to the Spirit, the things of the Spirit. For if you are living according to the flesh, you must die; but if by the Spirit you put to death the deeds of the body, you will live." (Rom. 8:5, 13)

Notice that Paul does not describe a mysterious feeling, but a mindset. Those who are "according to the Spirit" set their minds "on the things of the Spirit." The Holy Spirit does not bypass the mind; He renews it by means of the Spirit-inspired Word. As the believer understands and embraces that Word, he "puts to death the deeds of the body." The Spirit is the divine power, but He works through the truth He has already revealed in Scripture.

The Spirit's Role and Our Effort

Scripture often pictures spiritual growth with agricultural imagery. A farmer does not produce life; God does. Yet the farmer must labor if he expects a harvest. In the same way, no Christian can produce the fruit of the Spirit by sheer willpower, and yet no Christian grows without effort.

"Poor is he who works with a negligent hand, but the hand of the diligent makes rich." (Prov. 10:4)

A lazy farmer will not see fruit, even though sunshine and rain are available. Likewise, a spiritually negligent believer—who rarely reads, studies, or applies Scripture—will not see much of the Spirit's fruit in his life. The Holy Spirit has provided the perfect, inerrant Word; our responsibility is to respond diligently to that Word.

The Water of Truth and the Spirit's Work

Isaiah uses the language of thirst and water to describe God's gracious invitation:

"Ho! Every one who thirsts, come to the waters; and you who have no money come, buy and eat. Come, buy wine and milk without money and without cost." (Isa. 55:1)

The "waters" are the life-giving truth that God gives freely. The New Testament makes clear that this truth has now been inscripturated in the sixty-six books of the Bible, which are "inspired by God and profitable for teaching, for reproof, for correction, for training in righteousness" so that the man of God may be "equipped for every good work" (2 Tim. 3:16-17).

If we want the Spirit's fruit, we must continually "come to the waters" of Scripture. The Spirit does not give fresh revelation today, nor does He whisper extrabiblical messages into the believer's heart. Rather, He uses the once-for-all, inerrant Word that He inspired to supply everything needed for life and godliness. To neglect that Word is to neglect the very means by which the Spirit works.

Growing in Understanding: Study as a Means of Cultivation

Most believers do not read Hebrew or Greek, and yet the Spirit has providentially supplied faithful translations and the work of conservative textual scholars so that Christians can reliably access the meaning of the original text. The task, then, is not to wait for an inner flash of insight, but to engage the text carefully and reverently.

Christian leaders throughout church history have used tools such as lexicons, grammars, Bible dictionaries, and conservative commentaries—not to override Scripture, but to understand it more accurately. Likewise, individual believers can deepen their grasp of God's Word by reading good study Bibles, doctrinally sound resources, and by paying attention to context, grammar, and historical background. This is not "academic distraction"; it is one of the primary ways we cooperate with the Spirit's work of illumination.

As Peter notes, even the prophets themselves "sought and searched carefully" regarding the salvation later announced to us (1 Pet. 1:10-12). If inspired prophets had to study diligently, how much more should we?

Prayer and Dependence on the Father

Bible study alone does not cultivate the Spirit's fruit. It must be joined with prayerful dependence. Jesus taught:

"If you then, being evil, know how to give good gifts to your children, how much more will your heavenly Father give the Holy Spirit to those who ask Him?" (Luke 11:13)

As this book has argued, this is not a promise of a fresh, direct, apostolic-level bestowal of miraculous gifts. Rather, the Father delights to give the blessings of the Spirit's work to those who sincerely ask—chiefly through a deeper grasp of, and obedience to, the Spirit-inspired Scriptures.

Prayerful cultivation means we come to the Word asking the Father to help us understand, to humble our hearts, to expose our blind spots, and to strengthen our wills to obey. We are not asking for a new revelation, but for a new responsiveness to the revelation He has already given.

Cultivating the Fruit of the Spirit in Daily Life

Cultivating the Holy Spirit is not isolated from ordinary decisions. It is worked out in the million small choices of everyday life. When Scripture says the fruit of the Spirit is love, joy, peace, patience, kindness, goodness, faithfulness, gentleness, and self-control, it is describing traits that must be consciously practiced in concrete situations.

A believer who knows that Scripture commands forgiveness must choose, in reliance on God's help, to forgive rather than nourish bitterness. A believer who reads that anxiety should be replaced with prayer and thanksgiving must actually bring cares before God and meditate on His promises. In each case, the Holy Spirit uses the implanted Word to reshape responses, and over time, the pattern of life begins to match the pattern of Christ.

This is why Paul can say, "If we live by the Spirit, let us also walk by the Spirit" (Gal. 5:25). The same Spirit who gave life through the gospel now directs the steps of those who submit their minds and wills to Scripture.

The Role of Christian Community in Spirit-Governed Growth

The Spirit does not cultivate fruit in isolation. He uses the local congregation, where the Word is read, preached, taught, sung, and applied. Hebrews calls believers to "consider how to stir up one another to love and good works" and warns against "neglecting to meet together" (Heb. 10:24-25).

In corporate worship, Bible classes, and informal fellowship, the Spirit presses His Word into our hearts through the voices and examples of other believers. Rebuke, encouragement, correction, counsel, and comfort—all grounded in Scripture—are instruments He uses to prune and strengthen us, so that we may bear more fruit.

Conclusion: A Lifelong, Word-Driven Cultivation

To "cultivate the Holy Spirit" is not to chase ecstatic experiences or to wait for a mystical feeling of indwelling. It is to present ourselves daily to God, with open Bibles and dependent hearts, asking Him to use His Spirit-inspired, inerrant Word to renew our minds, subdue our flesh, and produce in us the fruit that reflects Christ.

This cultivation is lifelong. It involves diligent study, honest self-examination, persistent prayer, and active participation in the life of the church. As we do so, the Holy Spirit faithfully uses the Scriptures to guide, correct, strengthen, and transform us—so that our lives increasingly display the character of the One whose Word He breathed out.

Bibliography

Andrews, E. D. (2016). *EXPLAINING THE DOCTRINE OF SALVATION: Basic Bible Doctrines of the Christian Faith.* Cambridge, OH: Christian Publishing House.

Andrews, E. D. (2016). *INTERPRETING THE BIBLE: Introduction to Biblical Hermeneutics.* Cambridge, OH: Christian Publishing House.

Andrews, E. D. (2016). *YOUR WORD IS TRUTH: Being Sanctified In the Truth.* Cambridge, OH: Christian Publishing House.

Andrews, E. D. (2017). *HOW TO STUDY YOUR BIBLE: Rightly Handling the Word of God.* Cambridge, OH: Christian Publishing House.

Andrews, E. D. (2023). *BIBLICAL EXEGESIS: Biblical Criticism on Trial.* Cambridge, OH: Christian Publishing House.

Andrews, E. D. (2023). *UNSHAKABLE BELIEFS: Strategies for Strengthening and Defending Your Faith.* Cambridge, OH: Christian Publishing House.

Andrews, E. D. (2024). *CHRISTIAN THEOLOGY: The Christian's Ultimate Guide to Learning from the Bible.* Cambridge, OH: Christian Publishing House.

Andrews, E. D. (2025). *A FRESH LOOK AT PAUL'S THEOLOGY: Biblical Theology as Revealed through Paul.* Cambridge, OH: Christian Publishing House.

Andrews, E. D. (2025). *BIBLICAL WORDS AND THEIR MEANING: An Introduction to Lexical Semantics.* Cambridge, OH: Christian Publishing House.

Andrews, E. D. (2025). *EARLY CHRISTIANITY: Exploring Backgrounds, Historical Settings, and Cultures.* Cambridge, OH: Christian Publishing House.

Andrews, E. D. (2025). *IMMORTALITY OF THE SOUL: The Birth of the Doctrine.* Cambridge, OH: Christian Publishing House.

Andrews, E. D. (2025). *LINGUISTICS AND THE BIBLICAL TEXT: Unlocking Scripture Through the Science of Language.* Cambridge, OH: Christian Publishing House.

Andrews, E. D. (2025). *THE GUIDE TO SPIRITUAL WARFARE: Standing Firm in the Armor of God Against the Schemes of the Devil.* Cambridge, OH: Christian Publishing House.

Andrews, E. D. (2025). *UNDERSTANDING BIBLICAL WORDS: A Guide to Sound Interpretation.* Cambridge, OH: Christian Publishing House.

www.ingramcontent.com/pod-product-compliance
Lightning Source LLC
Chambersburg PA
CBHW071320090426
42738CB00012B/2743